Sharon Randall started as a part-time file clerk in the library of the *Monterey County Herald* in 1982 and became a feature writer in 1986. In April 1991 she began writing "Bay Window," a personal column of essays and observations on life and ordinary things.

Born in Hendersonville, NC, Randall grew up in Landrum, SC. For the past 33 years she has lived on the Monterey Peninsula in a 90-year-old house that is under constant renovation.

Her training to be a columnist, she says, included 15 years as a feature writer, 30 years as a wife and mother, and 50 years as a daughter, a sister, and a friend. A winner of numerous national awards for writing, Randall notes that she has also scrubbed a lot of toilets, washed a lot of towels, and burned a lot of cookies.

Since 1994, she has been a full-time syndicated columnist, writing twice weekly for the *Monterey County Herald* and Scripps Howard News Service with distribution to some 400 newspapers around the country. She is also a frequent speaker before civic and professional groups and charities.

Birdbaths
and
Paper Cranes

—

A Family Tale by
Sharon Randall

Foreword by her son, Josh Randall
Edited by Scott Brown, *Monterey County Herald*

A PLUME BOOK

For Randy

PLUME
Published by the Penguin Group
Penguin Putnam Inc., 375 Hudson Street, New York, New York 10014, U.S.A.
Penguin Books Ltd, 80 Strand, London WC2R 0RL, England
Penguin Books Australia Ltd, Ringwood, Victoria, Australia
Penguin Books Canada Ltd, 10 Alcorn Avenue, Toronto, Ontario, Canada M4V 3B2
Penguin Books (N.Z.) Ltd, 182-190 Wairau Road, Auckland 10, New Zealand

Penguin Books Ltd, Registered Offices: Harmondsworth, Middlesex, England

10 9 8 7 6 5 4 3 2 1

Text Copyright © *Monterey County Herald* and Sharon Randall, 2001, 2002
Illustration Copyright © K. L. Darnell, 2001
All rights reserved

 REGISTERED TRADEMARK—MARCA REGISTRADA

CIP data is available.
ISBN 1-58536-077-5 (hc.)
ISBN 0-452-28369-8 (pbk.)

BOOKS ARE AVAILABLE AT QUANTITY DISCOUNTS WHEN USED TO PROMOTE PRODUCTS OR SERVICES. FOR INFORMATION PLEASE WRITE TO PREMIUM MARKETING DIVISION, PENGUIN PUTNAM INC., 375 HUDSON STREET, NEW YORK, NEW YORK 10014.

Acknowledgments

—

To my editors—Tom Walton for hiring me; Will Smith for encouraging me; Pat Griffith for making me a feature writer; Mary Barker, Fred Hernandez, Mark Whittington, and Jeffrey Whitmore for making me a better writer; Reg Henry for making me a columnist; Walter Veazey for putting my columns on the wire; Scott Brown for putting them into this book; and Brian Lewis at Sleeping Bear Press for making the book a reality—I am grateful.

To a childhood friend—who forgave me in fifth grade when I accidentally bit her on the nose, and in high school, when I stole her boyfriend—I am grateful and very sorry.

To other friends, whom I have never bitten or stolen from—and who still call to see how I am doing even when I forget to call them—I am grateful and will try to call soon.

To the "Glee Club"—a group of women with whom I meet each week to pray and share confidentially from our lives—I am grateful, especially for all the material for a book.

To the people who read what I write—and who occasionally write back to offer their encouragement—I am grateful and forever in your debt.

And finally to my family, near and far, here and gone, most especially to my children—Nan and Nate, Josh and Claire—I am grateful beyond all words.

Foreword

by Josh Randall

———

I was going into fifth grade the summer my mom started working in the library of the *Monterey County Herald,* our local newspaper. She was 34, had three kids (my sister was 8, and our kid brother was 5), and had only two years of college education. All she wanted was a part-time job, something to offset my dad's modest teaching salary, now that we were all in school.

What we didn't know then and never could have guessed was that it was the first in a series of fateful steps that would one day land her a job with a description that goes something like this: Twice a week, put the details of your personal life—along with those of your husband, your dog and in particular, your three children—in print, any way that you see fit, for the world to read.

But we didn't know that at the start. We were just worried that if she went to work, our dad might have to do some of the cooking. Mostly, we were proud of her. For a poor Southern girl who came from a family without a college graduate, this would be, in short, unexpected and monumental. But we were always proud of her, our mom, even when she was just working for us for free—or as she put it, for love, instead of money.

She wrote her first short story for the Sunday magazine. It was about a Christmas when she was a little girl, and her brother, who was blind, was shooting caps by smashing them with a rock. She even drew the illustrations, with a little girl that looked sort of like my sister. My mom was surprised when she won an award for that story. I wasn't surprised at all. She was my mom—the one who showed up for all my games and cheered too loud—but I had a feeling that she could write. We all did. Even some of my friends. Most anybody with the ability to read could see it, including, importantly, the editors at the *Herald*.

While I was working my way through middle school, she was writing features and collecting more awards. And by the time I was finishing high school, she was also writing a column. She called it "Bay Window" in reference to the big glass lookout in the main bedroom that my dad had built over the family room in the house. The window, which had a view of both Monterey Bay and our backyard, was one of her favorite spots. It was the place where she daydreamed, stargazed and read to us for hours from books like *Rikki-Tikki-Tavi* and *The Narnia Chronicles*. The place where she sat to watch us and our friends build forts and play basketball and, in general, grow up.

Over the years, my sister and brother and I watched proudly, if not curiously, as the around-town reputations of our mother and father began to flip-flop: Once known as the "Coach's Wife," she became "The Writer"; and my dad, once "The Coach," became "The Writer's Husband." This change seemed to crystallize, in our minds anyhow, when her column was syndicated to over 400 newspapers and suddenly she was getting fan mail from around the country. As far as we could tell, our dad actually enjoyed it. He didn't seem to mind showing up in the paper and getting ribbed unmercifully by his students and fellow teachers. Then again, I suppose coaches are used to that.

As kids, we weren't sure what to make of it all. It was rumored, however, that there might be a pay raise involved, and we spent a good deal of time speculating out loud and discussing among ourselves when and how we might be compensated, fairly, as subjects of her work. For the record, we never saw a dime.

It's a mixed blessing, being the child of a writer—especially the child of a columnist working with the sort of grand and sweeping freedom that my mom seemed to enjoy. On one hand, we could open up the paper and see our names in print. On the other hand, we could arrive at school only to have our friends, teachers, and, occasionally, total strangers ask us to verify whatever she had chosen to write about us that day. Example: "Did you really sleep in your mom's bed until you were 6 years old?"

When we introduced her to our friends, they would say, "Your mom is really nice," and we would say, "Yeah, she is, but be careful what you say around her. It could end up in print."

Somewhere along the line I began to think of my mom not so much as a writer, but more as somebody who regularly made known to the public the details of my personal life: my eating habits; my occasional deficiencies in hygiene; my childhood affinity for shooting peas out of my nose.

If there was ever any real writing going on by her, I was sure it ranked only second to her primary goal, which was exposing, almost detective-style, the things I would rather not have exposed.

She was also prone to use what some might describe as "creative license," coming up with little tidbits about me and my family that were, I suppose, funny to read about, but not entirely accurate. Little embellishments.

Nothing big. Just a word or two. But when you're a teenager, it is not an enjoyable thing to find yourself misquoted, using expressions like "neato burrito." She swears that I said it. I assure you I did not.

While I have the chance, I might also add that I have done my own laundry since the age of 17, despite the implications of certain columns.

I am almost 30 now. I came home recently to find my wife, Claire, absorbed in reading from a stack of my mom's columns. There were 75 or so that Mom had sent when she asked me to write an introduction to her first book, one that will have, appropriately, a family theme.

Claire was moved to find her birthday column included in the bunch.

"I didn't know she was going to use that one," she said.

"Why wouldn't she?" I said. "As far as she's concerned, she's got herself another child in you."

I had read most of those stories before. They had arrived over the years, one by one, in my mailbox, on my computer screen, in my birthday cards. They always made me feel at home, wherever I happened to be. What was new to me now was having a stack of them in front of me, all arranged by their writer in a specific order. I read the first, then the second, and so on.

That's what she does for you, the reader, with this arrangement of stories. Each one stands on its own, but delivers you to the next.

As I moved from story to story, a momentum started to build, and I began letting go of the old misgivings and embarrassments that in the past, at times, had gone hand in hand with being written about. I found myself reading my mother's words simply for the pleasure of doing so.

When I finished, I noticed my wife was watching me.

"What is it?" she asked. (I can't hide anything from her.)

What it was, is that I was overwhelmed, feeling a sort of new and profound connection to my family, generations of people, alive and dead, scattered about the edges of the country, in the South and the West, and sewn together with a common thread.

"Do you know what you have there?" she said.

I let her continue.

"That's the greatest testament to love any mother could give."

As is often the case, she was right.

It was also, I realized, a testament to all families, and the relationships that bind them. And that is the book that you hold in your hands right now. It's a sampling from 10 years of writing about love and family by a fine and truly enjoyable writer—who also happens to be my mother.

Preface

—

I was born into a family of storytellers. Summers in my childhood were spent on the porch of my grandparents' cracker-box house in the mountains of North Carolina, where the only pastime—aside from slapping mosquitoes with one hand and pinching your cousins with the other, all the while pushing the porch swing with your toe—was telling stories and hearing them told. We did that all year round, really, but sometimes, depending on the weather, we moved it inside by the fire.

Like most Southern children, I learned early on how to be still and listen, not just with my ears, but with all my senses, and my very being. And as I listened, I began to see that every good story—like every good life—has a beginning, a middle, and an end. I got so good at spotting them I could see them coming like a train down the track.

My grandmother's stories would take your breath away, would cause the hair to bristle on your neck. She could summon wolves to the door, raise spirits from the dead, conjure up distant images and make them dance before your eyes, with just the wave of her hand and the lift of her brow and the power of her words. I always knew when she was about to tell a story because it would light up her eyes with an unmistakable gleam, a spark of mischief and mystery that her husband called "the devil."

Lord, I loved to see that.

My mother's life was a story in itself, an ongoing saga that always kept her searching somehow, and failing to find a happy ending. I could predict when she was about to add another chapter, because she would pack us up and take us home to stay, for a while, with her mother.

I knew when my blind brother was going to make me get up and tell him about the sunrise—a story he had already written in his mind but wanted me to put into words—because I would hear him at daybreak shuffling his feet and feeling his way in the dark to my room.

I could even tell when my grandfather—a sometime Baptist preacher who, as my grandmother liked to say, worked for the Lord when he couldn't find a paying job—was finally getting to the end of his sermon. He would lower his lovely baritone voice and pause for effect, then deliver a rousing altar call. By then, of course, the shouting would all be over and the congregation would have long since gone home.

Those stories and a thousand others flapped around in my head, hovering at the edges of my memory and imagination, like the shadows that fly after birds. I listened for their beginnings and middles and ends as a way of seeking order in chaos. You might say it was my obsession. I prefer to call it a preoccupation. Either way, any story, every story, real or imagined, mine or yours, I wanted to know it, then tell it in my own words.

It never occurred to me that I would earn my living writing. In school, my teachers often said I was a writer. They also said that I was chatty and lazy, but I liked writer best.

I had no idea what "writer" meant. I knew writers were people who wrote things, but I didn't know any of those people personally. Women in my family worked as mill-hands or waited tables, or they sat on the porch telling stories and shelling peas.

Getting paid to tell stories was nearly as unimaginable as hiring somebody else to shell the peas.

My senior year of high school, I kept praying for a miracle that would help pay my way to college. It came just before graduation when I won a scholarship after a deacon in my church signed me up, paid the fees and made me take the test.

Two years later, I decided to drop out of school, leave my family in the South, move to California, marry a high school basketball coach and, soon after, start a family. It sounded even to me like a harebrained plan, but it turned out to be the best decision of my life.

I had three babies in five years, taught Sunday School, washed towels for my husband's basketball team, read *Goodnight Moon* several thousand times and burned a lot of cookies. When my youngest child entered kindergarten, I took a part-time job as a file clerk in the library of the local newspaper, now the *Monterey County Herald*, and wrote freelance pieces for a couple of years until I was offered a job writing features.

"No, thanks," I said, "my kids are still little. I don't want to work full-time."

So they let me write part-time until 1990, the year my oldest left home for college.

In April 1991, when my editor called me into his office, I knew I was in trouble.

"I'm really sorry about yesterday," I said. "My daughter needed a ride to cheerleading practice and my husband wouldn't answer the phone in the gym. I swear I will never leave early again—after today when I have to sell hot dogs at my son's baseball game."

"Fine," he said, "but I want you to start writing a column."

Talk about putting the fear of God into you.

"Be serious!" I said. "I only left early once—or twice—this week!"

"I *am* serious," he said. "Think about it."

I thought about it all evening through 13 innings of baseball, and by the time the game was over, I wasn't sure who had won or lost, but I knew the sort of column I wanted to write.

My grandmother always said, "Never pretend to be what you aren't, or to know what you don't know." I decided that if I had to write a column, I would write about everyday people and ordinary things—family and friends, happiness and heartache, love and loss, and life and such. Things I was. Things I knew.

I began with a story about how my grandmother and my blind brother taught me how to see the world, and I promised readers that in future columns I would take a good look at whatever came my way and try to write about what I saw.

That was 10 years ago. I'm not sure I could have made that promise had I known then all I know now. But writing is like living. You don't always need to know the middle or the end; you just start at the beginning and take it as it comes. And that's what I did.

I wrote about my daughter, Joanna, who begged me when she was 2 to come have "tea" with her, and at 18, told me to get a life. And my youngest, Nate, who once tried to smuggle his "blankie" into kindergarten, and at 21, took off alone to go trekking in Nepal. And my oldest, Josh, who had big dreams of being a real cowboy someday, and instead grew up to be, not a real doctor, exactly, but he plays one on TV.

I wrote countless memories of growing up in the South in a big, crazy family, not much bigger or crazier than yours. I recalled how my blind brother got drunk once and tried to drive. How my baby brother, "Monkey Boy," tried his best to drown me. How my sister lost her wig in the bumper car arena. And how I got in big trouble with my mother for taking my husband and teenage children to see the Rolling Stones.

I wrote about my grandfather's preaching, my grandmother's scheming, my mother's pocketbook, my stepfather's loneliness, and my father's suicide.

I wrote about seasons and holidays, camping in summer, skiing at Christmas, keeping score at my husband's basketball games, and watching him battle for his life.

In April 1994, I was sitting by his bedside in the hospital waiting for him to wake up after surgery for cancer, dreading the moment when I would have to tell him that the news was even worse than we had feared. As I sat there watching him sleep like a baby, I kept asking questions that only God could answer: How was I going to tell my husband that he might have as little as six months to live? And how was I going to do all the things I would need to do—be with him for chemo and radiation and countless trips to the hospital, see that our children stayed healthy and whole, keep our home and our lives in some semblance of order, and try somehow to hang onto my job?

I was still asking "How?" and "Why?" when the phone beside my husband's bed rang so loud I jumped. It was my editor calling to tell me that my column was going to be syndicated. I would write twice a week from home or wherever I happened to be—even, on occasion, from my husband's hospital room—and my work would be distributed to newspapers all around the country.

It was not an answer to every prayer, but like candles on an altar, or fireflies on a lake, it shed enough light to make some things clearer and others easier to bear. I would remember that moment and the thought that filled it, years later, reading a card from a friend that said, "Barn's burnt down...now I can see the moon."

For 10 years, twice each week, I have been writing about the ordinary people and everyday things that fill my head with stories and my life with adventure—that make me want to wake each morning just to see who will show up and what will happen next.

It is always a surprise—especially when I hear from readers who write or phone or E-mail to say that my stories are their stories, too. Imagine that. We are far more alike than we are different—all of us—in the everyday matters of the heart.

This book is a collection of stories written over a period of 10 years. Each one stands alone to tell its own tale. But collectively, fit together like the pieces of a puzzle, they all tell the tale of a family.

I would hope that in these pages—in all the joys and none of the sorrows—that you might catch a few glimpses of your family, too, and begin to tell stories of your own.

If you do, be patient. The stories of a lifetime are not easily told. You never know who will show up or what will happen next. The greatest risk from the start is that, if you worry too much about how it will end, you can miss a lot in the middle.

As a child, I learned that every good story has a beginning, a middle, and an end. As a writer, I break them up into little pieces and put them back together like a puzzle. But as a woman, I am trying to learn to let the story unfold—to remember the beginning, and enjoy the middle, and find the grace to trust for the end.

I'd like to learn to do that before my story is over.

I suspect you might like to do that, too.

I wonder.

Do you think we will?

A Beginning

April 23, 1991 to April 10, 1994

—

A Middle

June 19, 1994 to September 3, 1997

—

An End...and A Beginning

February 15, 1998 to May 24, 2001

—

A Beginning

—

April 23, 1991 to April 10, 1994

Writes of Passage

– April 23, 1991 –

Two people come to mind as I write this, for reasons I hope to make apparent. Both rank high on my list of the 10 most stubborn individuals ever to be set loose upon the face of the Earth—along with my husband, three children, several coworkers and a dog. And both had a hand in helping to shape the way I look at the world.

In her later years, when the highlights of her life had long been recorded in the family Bible, my grandmother liked to pass the time at a lace-curtained window in her living room.

The window looked out on the main street of one of the countless small towns cradled in the Blue Ridge Mountains of North Carolina.

A window may seem like a rather dull companion for a woman as inquisitive as my grandmother. But if you read *To Kill a Mockingbird*, or other tales of small towns, you might know why it held her.

I can see her still, keeping watch at that window, rocking back and forth, side to side, heel to toe, hands clasped behind her back for balance; an egg-shaped body on two spindly legs, bosom melted onto belly, exhausted by too many years of hard work and far too many babies.

"Look at that," she would say, of someone who dared drive by her window at too great a speed, or walk by in too short a skirt. "Did you ever see such in your life?"

She didn't always require an answer, but the proper response, I learned, was "No ma'am, I surely never did."

My grandmother's front window vigil, as my grandfather called it, was her way of keeping an eye on the world.

What she saw there, or from the porch when weather permitted, might bring her pleasure or pain, delight or disgust, anger or amusement. Or it might be something quite ordinary, but worth a closer look.

In any case, she kept watch and told us what she saw. And if, at times, we differed with her assessments, we never once doubted her intentions, which were simply to call it as she saw it.

As a child, my brother practiced willfulness the way some children practice piano, and he has played it to his advantage ever since. Born blind and with a few other inconveniences that would slow, but never stop him, Joe took on the world like a heavyweight champion forced to defend his title with one hand behind his back.

He surprised several doctors by learning to walk, though he waited until the age of 5 to do it. It was more of a shuffle, really, than a walk. And it would get him into trouble at the school for the deaf and the blind, for beating up on the deaf boys who made the serious mistake of telling him he walked like Frankenstein.

But such as it was, Joe's shuffle meant freedom. He could push his tricycle far out into the field by our house, after dark, and into ditches whenever and wherever he pleased. Freedom. Joe liked it a lot. And once he had a taste of it, he seemed to resent help of any kind, with one exception: He asked that I be his eyes.

You might think it a privilege to be somebody's eyes, but I was 9 years old and did not. Like most brothers, blind or otherwise, Joe could be a real pain.

From the time he was about 6, maybe 7, he would get up before dawn to watch the sunrise. He couldn't see it, of course, but he could feel it, warming his face through the kitchen window.

That in itself was fine—a little unnatural, maybe, but harmless enough as long as he was quiet. But some mornings, Joe would come shuffling into my room just before the sun came up, to make me get up and tell him what it looked like.

And if my description of that sunrise fell short of his expectations, he would say, nope, that's not it, try again.

It would make me really mad.

But I would try again and again, until either I got it right, or got so surly that he would back off and leave me alone. Or until he needed to see something else.

In time, it became a game. I would describe something to Joe, in exchange for his describing something to me. And if his description fell short of my expectations, I'd say, nope, that's not it, try again.

And it would make him really mad.

A friend of mine who once heard that story said my brother made me a writer.

I don't know about that.

What I do know is that, like my grandmother, I love to take a good look at things and tell people what I see. It's what I hope to do each week with this new column of mine.

I'm old enough to know now that such a chance is a privilege. So if I fall short of your expectations, I'll count on you to tell me. If you don't, my brother probably will.

Mom's the Word

- May 7, 1991 -

I knew he would leave me someday.

But I didn't know it would seem so soon. Time is tricky. Look at it from one end, it stretches to infinity; look at it from the other, and wonder where it went. I figured 18 years would be about as much as I could count on. But when you're 23, 18 years seems like forever. Long enough to do anything. Even to watch a baby grow up to be a man.

My mother often said that with children, you have to take what time you're given and be glad for the memories. I told her she made it up so I'd feel guilty and sit on the porch with her when she got old. Fine, she said, I could make fun of her, but someday I'd have a child.

He was born January 27, 1972, during the first quarter of a basketball game that his father was supposed to coach but didn't.

He came into my life by invitation, and despite what my husband claims I said during labor, he was a most welcome guest. But what surprised me about his arrival (aside from the episiotomy) was how he seemed to know, without being told, that I was the hostess for this trip.

He had these fat little fingers, like a King Kong action figure, tiny but huge, that would clamp onto some part of me and refuse to let go until he pleased.

And when he was really hungry, which was basically all the time, just the sound of my voice would cause him to turn his face like a swimmer, from side to side, in a frantic but comical quest for food.

I'd never had that effect on anyone before and I found it flattering. But charmed as I was, I didn't fall at first sight. I waited until he opened his eyes.

They were blue, like his father's and my father's, too, and filled with all kinds of secrets. But what really got to me about this determined little alien, was seeing myself mirrored in his eyes and thinking I had never looked better.

So we struck a bargain, this baby and I, and it went something like this: I would give and he would take for as long as he should need me. I'd forsake all claims to freedom, forget the Bill of Rights, the ERA, and basic personal hygiene. I'd give up books, baths, sleep, socialization, and clothing that had to be dry-cleaned. I'd cross the bridge and torch it behind me, forever to be somebody's mother, and never again just somebody's little girl.

And in return, he would call me Mom.

Say I'm easy, but it seemed fair at the time. Then my "half" of the bargain began to kick in and I turned into a dairy.

Actually, the dairy business proved to be a godsend, because the boy truly loved to eat. Every two hours, day and night, rain or shine, weekends, holidays, you name it. He loved doing other things, as well, but eating always came first.

Those early days passed slowly. The first three months lasted about three years. But once we both got the hang of things, time began to pick up speed. It slowed briefly, for the births of his sister and brother, and hit a few snags during puberty. But much of it passed like a home video set on fast-forward.

Next thing I knew, he was off to college, and I was left with 18 years' worth of memories of all the people he had been on his way to becoming a man.

For instance, there he is as a baby, crawling on the floor, eating lint and babbling "Dada" (it seemed he had also struck a bargain with his dad).

And a little boy, building forts and chasing lizards; wearing a cape, jumping out of trees, calling, "Mom, watch me."

And a big boy, shooting hoops with his dad. Fighting off girls and their cooties. Delivering papers in the pouring rain, pleading, "Mom, please help me."

And a young man—6 feet 2 inches tall, a 200-pound tower of self-reliance, his cootie-phobia long forgotten, grinning goodbye outside his dorm, silently mouthing, "Mom, send money."

I liked all those people. Every one of them. And I miss them now that they're gone. In fact, some days I'd give almost anything to get them all back for a while. But if I had to choose just one to keep around, no problem; I'd say give me who he is now. This one does his own laundry.

I kept my part of the bargain. I stayed through colic, chicken pox, stomach flu, and stitches. I survived Little League, PTA, and more basketball games than Kareem Abdul-Jabbar's hair. I even camped out in a tent in the dirt.

I taught him what he needed to make it on his own without me. And all things considered, I did a pretty good job.

So here I am facing Mother's Day without the person who first called me Mom. But it's OK. Really. I know I'll hear from him. Bargain or not, he still calls me Mom. Every Sunday. Collect.

Besides, that's how it is with children. You have to take what time you're given and be glad for the memories. And I will tell him all about that when he calls.

Auto Suggestion
- May 28, 1991 -

I don't think much about cars usually, as long as mine starts and keeps running. I can't even identify a car properly. Instead of make and model, I cite color and size.

So I was surprised recently to realize that what I was feeling—a vague sort of sadness, as if I'd lost an old friend—was all because of a car. A little green one.

In the summer of 1968, I left college in North Carolina for what was supposed to be a brief vacation in California. My mother was dead-set against it. But I'd be staying with her sister, whom she trusted, despite her having married That Man and moved off to Godforsaken California. So Mother relented and I left, against her better judgment—a point she always stresses in citing it as an example of why one should never ignore one's better judgment.

That Man (also known as Uncle Joe) met me at the airport in San Francisco, and on the drive home, kept talking about some engineer he knew at work—a nice guy, one heck of a golfer, who was not only single, but drove a Porsche.

I thought he said porch. All I knew about cars was what I learned from my dad, a veteran of WWII and a devout believer in Fords, who said any man who drove any other make—especially a German make—was a heathen not to be trusted with his daughter. But I knew by the way Uncle That Man said "Porsche," I was supposed to be impressed.

"Really?" I said, feigning interest. "What color?"

"Green," he said, grinning. "It's a beauty. And the guy's not so bad-looking either."

One year later, I rode away in that green beauty with its not-so-bad-looking driver while 200 wedding guests pummeled us with rice, and my mother and Uncle That Man duked it out on the church lawn.

At first, I saw the Porsche more as a foe than a friend. My husband had bought it new, his first car with his first money from his first job after college, and he treated it nothing short of first class. He spent hours washing and waxing it, or tinkering with its engine.

Once he suggested we work on it together. California born and reared, my husband had a lot to learn about Southern women. It was the first of many opportunities I'd have to enlighten him.

What bothered me most about the Porsche was not the time my husband spent with it after we were married, but the time he had spent with it before I was part of his life. I know it is silly to resent a car—especially when there are so many other things to resent in a marriage—but I was young then, immature, not half as smart as I am now. And I didn't know then what I know now, which is that he meant it when he said, "'til death do us part."

My grandmother suggested I make a marriage vow to myself, as she had done some 50 years ago. Hers was to never start doing anything she didn't plan to keep doing forever. Mine was simpler. I vowed to outlast the Porsche.

Meanwhile, my husband decided, rather than make a lot of money, he would teach high school and coach basketball. Pretty soon there were papers to grade and practices to run—not to mention a roof that leaked, a yard that grew weeds, and a wife who kept having babies—so he had little time left for the Porsche. And somehow, over the years, it gradually changed from being a great car, to a great old car, to just an old car.

But something else changed, too. The Porsche and I became friends.

It took me back to North Carolina to visit my family. It carried me to the hospital when I had my first child. Sixteen years later, it taught that child how to drive. And the sound of its engine growling when it brought the boy home late at night would make me smile, whisper "Thanks," and fall asleep.

So recently, when the Porsche finally died, body and soul, we weren't sure what to do.

Sentimental as always, my husband wants to junk it. The kids think we should buy a new one. And our friends suggested we turn it into a sofa, maybe, or a planter.

You don't do that to a friend. So we're going to keep it, and someday, when we have time and money, we're going to have it restored. My husband could do the work himself. Or who knows, maybe we could work on it together?

On second thought, he can do it himself. It was his before it was mine.

The Pact

- June 23, 1991 -

My grandmothers were about as different, one from the other, as any two women could be. One sang soprano, whistled it while she worked. The other sang alto, sultry and low. Neither of them sang especially well, but together, their voices found harmony in me.

Neta and Grace met in 1942, soon after the former's 15-year-old daughter ran off to marry the latter's 25-year-old son. I am told the meeting was civil, though not especially cordial. The one thing they could agree on, knowing their children as they did, was that the marriage did not have a snowball's chance in hell.

Why do mothers always have to see a heartache coming long before it knocks on the door? They knew their children's marriage was grief in the making. But they promised each other to pray long and hard, to do all they could to help it last.

And so began a lifelong pact between two remarkably dissimilar women, a silent but mutual agreement of the heart to make something good out of nothing. Between them was a strength sufficient to move a mountain, but it was not enough to keep my parents together. The marriage lasted eight years. When it ended, Neta and Grace continued their pact for the two things they still had in common: my sister and me.

I was two years old. It took no effort on my part, none whatsoever, to become both women's favorite granddaughter. (My sister claims she was the favorite, but trust me, I know better.) Their constant and abiding love for me was a gift, free and clear. It was also my first lesson in grace, and to this day, I count it a blessing.

From the time I learned to walk until I left for college, my favorite place on earth was with either of my grandmothers. As it happened, I spent much of my childhood with one or the other. I don't know whose house I loved more.

One lived in a small town, surrounded by people, where she could know all there was to know—who, what, when, where, and how much they paid for it.

The other lived on a mountain, surrounded by nature, where she could know all there was to know about plants and creatures and the changing of seasons, and the quiet reassurance of living close to the earth.

But here is how they really differed.

My mother's mother was a preacher's wife who seldom set foot in church. A mischievous woman, a steel magnolia, she wore white gloves to go shopping, played cards with abandon, and swore under her breath like a sailor. She loved her husband almost as much as she loved Jesus. But she could not abide, she said, certain members of the congregation, or any other fools who thought too highly of themselves.

Being with her was pure adventure and a whole lot of fun.

My father's mother was a farmer's wife who seldom left the farm except to go to church every Sunday. She traveled through the pages of *National Geographic*, and with the turning of leaves, the migration of geese, and her own vivid flights of imagination.

She kept a garden, hiked for miles to pick blackberries, read novels, wrote poetry, and painted sunsets on stones. She made everything better, from doll clothes to biscuits to loneliness.

Being with her was pure adventure and a whole lot of fun.

But growing up in the care of two such women had an odd effect on my nature. I inherited both women's characters, not necessarily their better traits. Like two sides of the same coin, both are who I am. But you never know which side will turn up.

It drives my husband and my children crazy.

I'm neither alto nor soprano, can't hit the high notes, can't touch the lows. But sometimes, when the music gets too hard for me to follow, the notes will start to dance, rearranging themselves, until I hear myself singing with an entirely different voice, a three-part harmony all my own. And it doesn't sound half bad.

Generations

- November 12, 1991 -

Just outside of Pisgah National Forest in the Blue Ridge Mountains of North Carolina there lies a quiet little community of small farms and aging homesteads that will one day be replaced by golf courses and video outlets and time-share condominiums.

It is not a question of whether it will happen; it is happening already. The old-timers have grown weary of trying to prevent it, and wearier still of trying to understand why their children seem to think it cannot happen soon enough.

There are four lanes on the highway where there used to be but two, and a restaurant that stays open day and night just up the road. They built a golf course and some condos by the river on what was believed to be the site of an old Indian village. Golfers have been known to find arrowheads there from time to time it is said, even when they weren't looking for them.

There is a subdivision sprawling over a hillside that, not so long ago, grew thick with dogwood and wild rhododendron and blackberries free for the picking, and another being built on some farmland where the barn will be left standing as part of the overall design because somebody thought it looked quaint.

But changes notwithstanding, it remains the same place in at least some of the ways that mattered most to me when I was growing up there a lifetime ago.

Buildings, even landscapes, may be altered overnight, but people and their customs take a bit more time to change.

I discovered that recently when I went back to North Carolina, "home" as they say, to bury my father.

If you get off the four-lane road and drive a short distance into those mountains, you will meet people whose families, like my father's, have lived there for generations.

Gentle by nature and proud to a fault, they usually suffer somewhat from being torn between a love for privacy and a curiosity for the world.

They have lovely given names such as Harlan and Lacy, and common family names that tie them like unbreakable threads to distant aunts and uncles and cousins, no matter how far removed.

Many of them still live on the same land where they played as children, often as not in the same house where they were born. No longer able to eke a living out of farming, they work indoors at textile mills and grocery stores and such, but they still tend gardens, both for vegetables and flowers. They grow the best corn and tomatoes you'll ever put in your mouth and chrysanthemums as big and golden as a baby's head.

If you have occasion to visit, don't be put off by their dogs. Hounds, mostly, they rouse themselves from a stupor and bark like they mean business when a stranger comes near. But they're good dogs, for the most part, and they generally don't bite. Tell them to hush and they will.

When the barking tells the people inside that they have company, they will come out on the porch to meet you, and call off the dogs if need be. And then they will invite you into their homes and inquire after your mother and offer you something to eat—every time without fail.

When you leave you'll be laden with vegetables from their gardens, fresh if in season, canned if not, and maybe some venison from their freezers. They'll tell you to come back to see them again soon, and you'll find yourself hoping you can.

That was the sort of people I knew when I was growing up, and got to know again last week after 20 years away.

They brought ham and potato salad and sweet potato pies, and made me laugh with much-embellished stories about my dad. Then they stood by my side as he was buried in the church cemetery where nearly all of them have laid loved ones to rest over the years.

Fall had come and nearly gone when I arrived there, I was told, but the colors of the leaves were still quite something to see. It was my favorite time of year when I lived there. Still is, for that matter.

When I was a child I was fascinated by the annual transformation, watching dark green slowly turn to scarlet and gold, then finally, inevitably, to brown. But I always had trouble with the last part of the process, when the leaves lay fallen in great crumbling heaps on the ground, and spring seemed so very far away.

My dad used to tell me that dying is a necessary part of life—that it's how old things fulfill their purpose and make room on the earth for the new.

Leaves have destinies of their own, I believe, that have little to do with us. We can no more prevent them from dying in autumn than we can cause them to bud in the spring. And so we rely on memories—green and scarlet and gold and brown—to see us through the winter. And most of the time, it is enough.

Tea 'Right Now'
- January 14, 1992 -

When our daughter, Joanna, was barely two years old, my husband went into hiding in his workshop, as he is wont to do, spending evening upon evening sawing and sanding and nailing and painting what would turn out to be the stuff of his little girl's dreams.

"Tove," she had told him, placing her Christmas order, "and pidgerator, too."

And so, on Christmas Eve, he emerged from his workshop, paint-splattered but proud, to present her with a miniature stove and matching refrigerator.

Made of wood and painted green, with real wire racks and doors that opened and tiny knobs that turned, they were state-of-the-art pretend technology, perfect for serving imaginary "tea."

During the next several years, "tea" was a ritual at our house. The menu and guest list varied according to the whim of the hostess, but the time at which she served it was always "right now."

Nan would bounce—or hop or dance or spin or roll—into the room and announce, hands on hips, "Time for tea, Mommy. Right now!"

That meant I was to drop whatever I was holding—a pot of spaghetti sauce or her baby brother—and report at once to her room. And I did so gladly, as often as possible, though in hindsight, not as often as I might have.

We would sit together, she and I (and often her baby brother) at a small table with her three favorite dolls, Amanda, J.J., and Elisabeth Claire. The dolls were required to dress for the occasion. Her brother and I usually came as we were.

Then she would pour "tea" for us and serve cookies, real or

imagined, and we would exchange pleasantries and discuss topics of mutual interest—such as, where (and in which neighbor's yard) did she find the flowers for her table?

She was tireless, sometimes hosting half a dozen "teas" a day for anyone willing to come "right now."

She would take her father by the hand and lead him, trailing sawdust from his workshop, to her room where he would sit obediently, like a bear on a bicycle, drinking "tea" from a tiny cup.

She would lure her big brother and his buddies in from a hard day at play by promising them real cookies and then lecturing them on etiquette.

She would dress up her baby brother in all sorts of outlandish attire and prop him up at her table. And if no one else was available "right now," she would serve "tea" to the dog, if she could catch him and wrestle him into a dress.

For a time, I let myself think that she would never tire of "tea." But tire she did, of tea parties and dress-up and other little-girl games. At the same time, she lost all vestige of interest in major household appliances.

So the green stove and refrigerator were stored in the garage until her parents were ready to part with them.

But even as our daughter was saying goodbye to little-girlhood, our friends' daughter was saying hello.

Soon after she was born, Caillie was found to have a rare heart defect that would require surgery before her birthday. By the time she was three, she had survived repeated heart failure, stroke, pneumonia, and other complications.

And through it all, thanks to her parents' determination to give her as "normal" a life as possible, Caillie got to be an accomplished hostess, with the sort of flair that reflected her fiery hair and blue eyes and irrepressible personality.

The green stove and refrigerator seemed right at home in the playhouse Caillie's dad built for her. She took excellent care of them, too, keeping them spotless and using them often to serve "tea" to anyone available "right now."

Two months before her fifth birthday, after two unsuccessful heart transplants, Caillie gave up the fight. She was mourned by family and friends, and by countless others, many who never met her, but felt the loss nonetheless.

Meanwhile, the green stove and refrigerator went into storage until her parents were ready to part with them.

That came recently, when Caillie's dad phoned to ask if he might return them. We talked for some time about our families. (They have two preschoolers, our three are almost grown.) We marveled at how busy, how good our lives seem. And we promised we'd try to get everybody together, maybe go camping, real soon.

So the green stove and refrigerator are back, looking a little dated, but as loved and priceless as any antiques.

I thought about storing them for future (gulp) grandchildren. But my friend Alison, who is three, loves to play hostess, so they're going to be hers for a while.

The future is for dreams, just as the past is for memories. But the only time for tea is right now.

Barbs of Youth

- January 21, 1992 -

Once, when I was very young, my grandmother told me she believed I would never intentionally do anything wrong. She was known to be a fine judge of character, but she sure missed the mark on me.

Of course, she never found out what happened that day when my brother got his leg caught in the barbed-wire fence and had to go get sewn up. It was the day Doc Miller learned to respect the strength of scared little boys, and I learned what it means to be forgiven.

Denton was five years old, a sweet, squirrely boy with trusting brown eyes whose only serious drawback was that he smelled like a dog with the mange.

I knew the smell because we had such a dog. Denton named him Speckles the day he arrived, meek and hairless, at our door. He loved that animal, mange and all, and clearly the feeling was mutual.

Not one to take disfiguring diseases lightly, my mother soaked poor Speckles in creosote and warned us to keep our distance until the dog showed signs of hair. But Denton played with him anyhow, racing him along the railroad tracks, rolling with him in the pasture. Which should explain, to some extent, why they both smelled as they did.

Smell or not, they were my only hope of companionship in that tenth summer of my life. We lived in the country, surrounded by peach orchards and pastures, miles from any of my friends.

My older sister had gone to live with our grandmother. And my brother, Joe, who was just a year older than Denton, was spending two months in Shriners Hospital having surgery and physical therapy that promised to help him walk.

So I was stuck that summer with a small boy and a mangy dog. (In all fairness, I suspect they likewise felt stuck with me.) At any rate, the three of us agreed to make the best of it, which turned out to be not much at all.

We made up a game, embarrassingly simple but entertaining nonetheless, taking turns jumping a barbed-wire fence. Actually, Denton and I took turns, each of us holding down the fence as the other jumped it, while Speckles just jumped it every time. We told him he needn't help with the holding, as long as he kept out of the way when we jumped, and he seemed to think it was fair.

We explored every possible variation on the game's original theme, amazing ourselves and even Speckles, at times, with each new personal best.

One steamy, hot day in August, I had just completed a particularly intricate jump with what I judged to be unusual grace, when it occurred to me, that had any of my school friends been around for my performance, I would have felt not proud, but foolish. Suddenly, I thought of a new twist for the game, one I was sure my friends would find hilarious.

Denton had already started his approach from about 50 yards away, with Speckles close on his heels. I held down the fence, as I had each time before, and watched as they drew closer, grew larger, as if in slow motion. Then, just as they both became airborne, I simply let go.

Speckles cleared easily. Denton did not. He lay motionless, sprawled on the ground, a six-inch gash oozing red from his leg, and Speckles licking his face.

I decided my brother was dead and started praying fervently to join him.

Suddenly, he began to scream.

I recognized it instantly as the most horrible, wonderful sound I had ever heard, and then I ran to get my mother.

We wrapped Denton's leg in a towel and carried him, kicking and screaming, to the car. My mother drove him to the doctor, leaving me all alone to face myself and seek comfort in a mangy dog.

As I waited for the police to come and put on the cuffs, I replayed the tapes in my mind, slowly, frame by frame, trying to understand what could have possessed me to betray my brother so. Finally, I knew. I had not done it to harm him; I had done it to get a laugh. And the thought of it made me physically ill.

Hours passed, the police never showed, and Denton came home a hero, showing off his stitches, boasting about how Doc Miller had gotten everybody in the waiting room to help hold him down.

I expected to be held accountable, to hear my brother tell the world what sort of person he had found me to be. But it never happened. Not then. Not since.

There was a look that passed between us—he knew, as I did, what had caused his pain—but in the next instant, it was gone.

Then he climbed into my lap, asked for a story, and promptly fell asleep. He still smelled like a mangy dog.

But for some reason, I rather liked it.

Singing for Ourselves
- February 18, 1992 -

She was born sixth in a family of 10 children that included nine girls—said to be blessed with the voices of angels—and one boy, who, if he had a voice, never got much chance to use it.

She sang neither alto nor soprano, just somewhere in between. If her voice lacked the strength to stand all alone, well, let it find harmony with those of her sisters' and it could stand any place it pleased.

My mother did not do everything well, but this much I'll give her: she could sing. So could her sisters. Everybody said so.

Actually, what they said was, "Those Wilde girls ought to be in radio; they could be somebody, for sure."

Wilde was the name, not their reputation, my grandfather would say with a wink. He was proud of his name, as he was of his daughters, but he didn't seem to mind joking about it. Seems he'd learned not to take life too seriously.

I guess any preacher named Wilde—especially one who married a mischievous woman and fathered nine headstrong girls and one tight-lipped boy—would need to seek salvation in a sense of humor as much as in the Good Book.

When the girls were young and still somewhat manageable, Preacher Wilde liked to have them sing in church.

They were called the "Cheerful Chimers" ("Wilde Girls" seemed a bit coarse for church) and they knew by heart every hymn ever sung.

But as the Chimers grew older and noticeably less cheerful, their interests strayed from hymns to "hims," just as their mother had predicted.

She had always been against having the girls sing for church; said it reminded her of a pony show at the circus. Surely the Lord would not be pleased to share his stage with a circus act, she said, no matter how talented the ponies.

Gradually my grandfather resigned himself to hearing his daughters sing only at home, whenever and whatever they pleased. That's when I came along.

My mother and most of her sisters married young and mothered early, leaving little time for singing. But when the family met for holidays or shared Sunday dinner—when they lingered on the porch on summer nights, or gathered by the fire in winter—someone would hum a note, as if on cue, and once again, the Wilde Girls would sing.

They sang hymns for my grandfather, and country for my grandmother, and sisters (as in Andrews and McGuire) for themselves, while my cousins and I played at their feet.

My memories of those evenings—chasing lightning bugs in the yard, or playing checkers on the floor—all sound much the same, with my mother and my aunts harmonizing in the background.

No one seems to recall exactly how it happened, but somehow they ended up on the radio. It was a local station, only one song a week. But it was radio just the same and, as everybody said, it was a surefire shot at being somebody.

Thing is, the studio was so small it could hold only four sisters, and it got to be a problem deciding which four of the nine it would be. At first they took turns, with my mother pretty much a regular, but gradually it turned into a fight.

They fought over who would sing, what to sing, how to sing it, even what to wear, which made no sense, given it was radio.

Finally, when they'd had their fill of fighting, they gave up trying to be somebody on the radio, and went back to being the Wilde Girls once and for all.

Years later, after my grandparents were gone and their grandchildren were grown and scattered, the family gathered at my mother's home following a funeral for the youngest sister, my favorite aunt.

It's hard on a family when the baby's first to go. You could see that in my mother and her sisters—the looks on their faces, the silences between them, more mournful than the gnashing of teeth and the tearing of hair.

Then someone (was that my sister?) hummed a note, as if on cue, and my cousins and I joined in.

We sang hymns for our grandfather, and country for our grandmother, sister songs for our mothers, who smiled, shaking their heads and tapping their toes in time to our singing.

We even did some Motown, just for us.

Ours were not the voices of angels. Certainly not my cousin Nick's. But we'd been blessed to hear angels singing in our childhood and we remembered enough to do a fair job of singing on our own.

Everybody said so. Besides, we weren't singing for the radio.

Picture Me a Miracle
- March 30, 1992 -

M y mother called my brother an Easter egg. He was hatched, she said, on Good Friday. His head actually looked like an egg, hardboiled and hairless, much like a fist with eyes.

He was the tiniest human I'd ever seen, barely three pounds at birth, and when he wrapped his spidery fingers around my thumb, I'd have gladly died to protect him.

I don't know how I remember all that, but I do, it seems, so clearly. Do we ever forget falling in love? He was six months old, crawling like a box turtle, when my mother told me he was blind.

"He can't be," I said. "He knows my face. He smiles at me all the time."

"No," said my mother. "He smiles at your voice. He will never see your face."

Her words rang with a finality that I didn't dare question further. Joe was blind. That was that. Could I be excused from the table now?

Children often are better than adults at accepting the unacceptable. Bitterness and self-pity rarely take root, it seems, in anyone, young or old, who keeps growing.

My brother grew slowly—too slowly, said the doctors—but with such fierceness for learning my head ached trying to answer his questions.

"Picture me this," he'd say, demanding that I describe something, anything that caught his interest, even things I'd never seen—the whirring of engines, the ticking of clocks, the whisper of angels in the trees.

I discovered that words are fickle, nothing but symbols for

the meanings we assign to them; otherwise, we'd all speak one language with never a misunderstanding.

When I couldn't find the right words, I would simply make something up. The color purple, for example, was thunder, deep and rolling. Red was hot chili peppers, made you sit up and think. Blue was the icy river where we learned to swim. It wasn't a language of precision, but it seemed to meet our needs. I gave him words for visions and he taught me how to see.

When I was 12 and Joe was 8, I asked God for a miracle. On Palm Sunday in church, I heard the preacher explain how the resurrection wasn't a one-time thing; that God performed miracles every day and all we had to do was expect them.

Maybe that was it, I thought. I had prayed for a miracle a million times, but never expected much.

"God," I said, "this Easter, I'll expect my brother to be able to see. Sorry I didn't expect it sooner."

I expected hard all week, twice as hard on Saturday, couldn't get to sleep that night. I heard my mother filling Easter baskets out in the kitchen. I thought of how happy she'd be about the miracle. I'd never have to wash dishes again.

Easter morning, when my brother was still blind as a bat, I almost, but not quite, lost my faith. I had never been in it for the miracles, and I wasn't about to bail out, but I will admit that I was sorely tempted to set the parsonage on fire.

"Are you sure you're still blind?" I said, waving a hand in Joe's face. "I asked God to give you eyes..."

"He did," Joe said. "He gave me yours. Can you see my Easter basket?"

Bobbie and Me
- September 22, 1992 -

We grew up together, she and I, shared a room and a double bed, and a big, boisterous family about as peculiar as any you'll ever meet. She was older than I by six years, or as she likes to say, five years and five months. She was bossy and I was bratty and we often fought like badgers. But many a time, I felt that it was just the two of us, Bobbie and me, me and Bobbie, alone against the world.

We were sisters and nobody, nothing came between us. At least, not for long. That's the way it was when we were growing up. And for some reason, that's the way we always thought it would be.

But then she got married and had babies. And I went off to college and ended up in California, of all places, alone and dependent upon the kindness of strangers some 3,000 miles away.

I've been back to visit her, of course, on numerous occasions, though mostly for funerals, I admit. But in the 23 years since she was matron of honor at my wedding, my sister politely declined repeated invitations to visit me in California. Too busy, too pregnant, too poor, you name it. Bobbie always had some sort of excuse. Until recently, that is, when she showed up and stayed put for two entire weeks.

It was a promise she had made to me last fall as we said goodbye in the airport two days after burying our father.

"I'm going to come out to see you," she told me, "this time, I swear, I really am."

"Right," I said laughing, "You bet."

I never thought I'd live to see it.

But for two weeks, there she was, Bobbie in the flesh. Sleeping on my Hide-A-Bed. Eating at my table. Smoking on my back porch. Listening to oldies on my radio. Laughing with my husband and children. Charming all my friends. And oh, yes, being my Big Sister.

Bossy as ever.

"What do you mean, you don't make iced tea?" she asked, reminding me of our Southern heritage, a grand old tradition of brewing iced tea by the gallon and deep-frying everything else in sight.

"Nobody in this house likes iced tea," I told her, "that's why I don't make it."

"They'll like it," she said sweetly, putting a pan of water on to boil, "if you make it the right way."

She, of course, made tea the right way, the way our mother always made it, bringing it just to a boil and then letting it steep until it was black enough to pass for coffee. But unlike our mother, who always added several pounds of sugar, more or less, before the tea cooled, my sister left it unsweetened, allowing others, she said, to "sweeten to taste."

Everybody at my house liked it.

In two short weeks, we drank enough iced tea to fill up an Olympic-sized pool.

We did other things, too, tourist kinds of things, trips to San Francisco and Big Sur, the 17-Mile Drive and Fisherman's Wharf, and every major shopping mall within 100 square miles.

But mostly, we remembered the times.

Like the time she got a beautiful bride doll for Christmas, and all I got was a tea set. Hence my aversion to tea.

Or the time she dressed up in a sheet and tried to scare that timid boy who lived up the road, and he in turn, nearly killed her with an ax.

Or the time she got to go to Florida to see Ross Allen's

Reptile Farm with Aunt Jane, Uncle Leroy, seven cousins, three dogs, several watermelons, and a monkey, while I had to stay home because there wasn't room in the pickup for one more.

Or the time her wig got knocked off in the bumper car arena, right there in front of me and God and all His Angels.

We talked about other times, too, good and bad, that we had weathered together.

Bobbie always seemed to have a way of knowing what I needed to hear. When we were little girls and our parents divorced, she convinced me it was for the better.

When I was seven and broke my brand-new front tooth, she held me and told me it could be fixed good as new, and that she wouldn't let the dentist hurt me.

When our baby brother was born blind, she said it wouldn't matter to anybody, except to people who didn't matter.

And last fall, when our dad took his life, she promised to come and see me.

And so she did. For two weeks, it was like old times, me and Bobbie, Bobbie and me. Then it was time for her to go.

Airports look different, I've noticed, depending on whether you are saying hello or goodbye. San Jose International had aged a lot in two weeks.

I don't care much for goodbyes, but Bobbie made this one easier. One quick hug and she was gone. Then suddenly she was back—looking just as she had when she lost her wig in the bumper car arena—to get the purse she left behind. Then she was gone again.

I stood there laughing as she ran to catch her plane.

Then I went home to make iced tea.

On Avery Creek
- October 13, 1992 -

Even now, after all these years, when I think of Avery Creek, I get angry all over again. In truth, what I feel is more akin to envy than to anger. Is it possible to be envious of a place you've never been? If so, then that's what I feel for Avery Creek.

My father and his brothers were mountain boys, born and raised on a small farm in western North Carolina, cradled from birth to manhood by the rolling valleys of the Blue Ridge.

From the time they could crawl, they studied the mountains—rocks and plants and animals alike—and committed them to memory, by sight and sound, taste and smell, by touch and instinct and heart.

They knew the land the way they knew their names, and for the same reason—so as to not forget who they were.

When they were old enough to go to school, they walked miles each day, or so they said, to a one-room school where they met—and fought and ultimately befriended—other mountain boys like themselves, though none as smart or handsome or strong.

Together they learned to read and write and cipher, and for the first time in their lives, they heard of faraway places with strange-sounding names, that they would one day defend—perhaps even die for—in a war half a world away.

They didn't know that then, of course. It probably never occurred to them that they'd ever have reason to leave home. When farming failed them as a means of livelihood, they settled for jobs they despised in textile mills, rather than set one foot off the mountains they loved.

They worked hard by day, slept soundly at night, and played

whenever they got the chance, which as they saw it, was not nearly often enough.

Given a choice, they might have played all the time. But choice is hard to come by for decent men with mouths to feed.

Still, they found ways (excuses, said their wives) for combining work with play.

Fishing and hunting—the games of their boyhood—became manly pursuits to put food on their families' tables.

Even when the families, not to mention their friends and neighbors, had quite enough trout and catfish and venison and bear meat to fill their tables for life.

Of all "modern" conveniences, next to a John Deere tractor and a Ford pickup truck—or even a copper kettle and coil—my dad and his brothers and all their old buddies loved the Deepfreezer best.

Keeping it filled gave them a perfect excuse to take off together, boys once again, to play to their hearts' content.

Most often, they went to Avery Creek.

To get there, they claimed, meant hiking for many miles, scaling granite cliffs, crossing raging rivers, facing unknown dangers at every turn.

Never once did I get to go along.

When I was young, they said I couldn't go because I was a little girl and one of them might end up having to carry me.

When I grew up, they said I couldn't go because they were old men, and I might end up having to carry one of them.

They had a big laugh over that, I'll bet.

They never let me go with them, and it always made me hopping mad. Yet I could not resist the stories they offered, like crumbs, when they came home.

To hear them tell it, Avery Creek was the most wondrous,

most adventurous, most rapturous place on earth.

At least, that's how I heard it. If it were not so all year-round, I thought, it was surely true when they were there.

They're all gone now—my dad and Uncle Charlie died just last year—following their lifelong friends, Horace and Glen, and several others whose names I can't recall.

Bear season will open soon anyway, without them, of course. And I suspect the bears are going to sorely miss the sight of a small band of half-blind, hobbling, toothless old boys, trying to pass themselves off as fearless hunters.

They were the sort of men who never asked for much in life, which is good because they never got much, either.

They went to war as boys and came back as men, then worked as mill-hands for 40 years or so until they had strokes or heart attacks, or simply got old.

They watched their children grow up and leave the mountains for the city.

They saw their farms being sold off and subdivided to build summer homes for rich Yankees.

And they never did get to see the Braves win the World Series.

But through it all—despite hardship and heartache, despite age and infirmity, despite hell and high water and who knows what else—they still managed, year after year, to have some good times together up on Avery Creek.

It still makes me mad, of course, to think I never got to go there with them. But I'll remember it, as I'll remember them—so as not to forget who I am.

Moonstruck

- March 9, 1993 -

My mother liked to say that I must have been moonstruck when I was a baby. It would explain, she said, a lot of my nature, though certainly not all. I always assumed she was teasing. With my mother, it was a safe assumption.

Still, I have to wonder. Moonstruck?

I did grow up with certain illusions about the nature and meaning of light. To be honest, I harbor some of them still.

There is in my memory—or possibly, in my imagination—a baby, fat and round, lying wide-eyed awake in her crib late at night, waiting for the moon.

I remember how still she lay, scarcely breathing, as she watched it coming toward her, gliding through the window, across the floor and over the railing, to lull her to sleep in its long arms.

Does the moon have arms?

Rest assured, it did then.

I never told my mother about that memory. She worried enough as it was.

I don't recall when I first saw a face in the moon, but in time, I came to know it about as well as I knew my own.

Pale and cool and quizzical, its expression never changed, and it looked directly at me, or so it seemed, as if to say, "What are you going to do about it"?

"What am I going to do about what?" I would plead, time and again, on balmy summer nights and steely winter mornings throughout much of my childhood. "What am I going to do about WHAT?"

But the moon, it never had an answer.

Are you relieved to hear that?

I was. At times, I didn't want an answer. Other times, I was peeved. I generally like to know what's expected of me.

Things grew worse as I got older.

When I was six, I noticed while driving with my family, that the moon would follow, playing hide and seek, darting between trees, winking at me with its golden eye.

Sometimes on warm nights, my cousins and I would give chase, running barefoot in a meadow bright with moonlight.

And always, if I stopped in my tracks and looked straight up, the moon would be looking at me. Just me. And the stars would be staring at me, too.

I didn't tell my mother about that, either, for fear she'd have me committed. And I sure as heck didn't tell my cousins.

Then the sun got in on the act.

The first time I noticed it was at Green River. I was seven years old, maybe eight.

While my brothers and cousins splashed silver in the shallows, I ventured out to float downstream on the current.

You guessed it. The sun followed after me, sending a wide shaft of light walking across the water to warm my face.

And when I went back upstream to float down once more, it followed me again, all the way, up and back.

I saw that phenomenon repeated countless times on rivers, lakes, even on the ocean. Over blue mountains and green valleys, across fields tall with corn and pastures deep with snow.

Light followed me wherever I went.

I couldn't believe nobody noticed it. And I couldn't help wondering, why me?

It scared me at first, to be so singled out. But in time, I found I rather liked it. A child who longs for attention will take it where she can find it, I suppose, even if only in the light.

Imagine my surprise years later in school when my teacher talked about optical illusions and the true nature and meaning of light. The face in the moon is not a face, she said, but a configuration of craters, vaguely resembling a face, perhaps, but only the random, thoughtless work of meteors.

What's more, she said, the moon has no light of its own to give, it merely reflects what it catches from the sun.

And the sun, yes, it gives light, she said, but it does so without thought or motive or preference, like a flashlight from afar.

Oh, I thought, so that's it.

To hide my dismay at this revelation, I nodded my head to my teacher's words, as if to say, "I knew that, yes, of course, I've known that all along." Though in truth, I'd known nothing of the kind.

Then I looked at the class and saw others nodding with me. And I realized maybe I was not the only one, after all, to feel singled out, sought after by the sun, moon, and stars. Who knows, I thought, maybe all children feel it. Maybe our teacher had felt it once, too.

So it is with growing up. We give the lie to childhood illusions, against our better instincts, and go in search of new light.

And yet sometimes still, when I can't sleep, I find my way to the window. And there in the moon, I still see a face, pale and cool and quizzical, as always, looking directly at me. Just me.

And it still wants to know what I'm going to do about it.

My Brother's Dream of Speed
- March 15, 1993 -

My brother had a driving passion for cars. So to speak. Fords in particular. He was especially fond of speed.

It was enough to make my mother fear that he was crazy. But she feared that about all of us, including herself.

When Joe was little, he'd say, "Sister, when I'm old enough to get my license, I'll fly so fast the angels will run and hide their wings."

Then he'd grin real big, picturing how it would be.

I could have told him it would never happen. No matter how old he got, he'd never get a license, never drive a car. But I didn't tell him that.

Joe was born blind. He couldn't see his own face in a magnifying mirror. But he could dream, yes he could, like nobody's business.

I had dreams of my own, things I hoped for, knowing I might never see them. What were the odds I'd get to go to college? Or earn my living as a writer? Or visit strange, foreign lands like California? I'd bet more money on my blind brother's chances of getting to drive at the Indy 500.

I didn't want to be the one to dim Joe's dreams. Life would do that soon enough. Until then, didn't he deserve a few happy anticipations?

What else was dreaming for?

Joe had trouble not just with his eyes but with his legs. He didn't walk until he was five. That's when he got his first "car," a red tricycle that he called his '49 Ford.

He couldn't pedal, so he'd push it, one hand on the seat, the other on the handlebars, driving daylight to dark, all around the yard, into ditches, anytime, any place he pleased.

Come bad weather, if our mother threw a fit big enough to

keep him inside, Joe would drive his other "Ford," a green, over-stuffed armchair. It had a few miles on it, he said, but it ran fine if you knew how to drive it. Which, of course, he did.

Growing up is a tug of war between disappointment and surprise, a reconciliation of dreams and reality. By the time he was 12, I think Joe realized he'd never get a license. He didn't mention it anymore.

As he had with other hard facts of life, he seemed to accept it without question, without bitterness, as if it were nothing more than a card drawn at random from a deck.

One summer day when he was 16, Joe went tapping out the driveway with his cane, click, click, and tapped into my stepfather's '49 Ford. He ran his hand along the hood, felt the heat of the metal, opened the door and climbed behind the wheel. He looked good.

Rummaging under the seat, he discovered a six-pack of Budweiser. It was so hot, he said later, that it burned the roof of his mouth. Maybe so, but he drained all six cans.

Then he felt along the steering column, found the keys in the ignition, shouted, "Hooweeee!" and fired it up.

To my grave, I'll regret that I didn't get to see it. By then, I was out of college, off in California, earning my living as a writer. I've heard various versions of the story, depending on the teller. They all boil down to this:

The Ford's engine roared.

My mother fainted.

My stepfather nearly killed himself running out the door.

And my brother, after a moment of pure bliss, threw up on the dashboard and the seat.

The Ford was up on blocks. It never moved an inch. But Joe swears he heard angels running to hide their wings.

One True Thing
- March 23, 1993 -

Looking back, I realize, all things considered, we probably never should have gotten married in the first place.

At least, not to each other.

As a couple, we had some serious strikes against us—major whiffs, actually—before we even got to bat. As a candidate for marriage, I was not what you'd call a sure thing.

I come from a long line of strong-willed women who married young and divorced early, only to marry and divorce again.

My grandparents had nine daughters and more sons-in-law than they could name. The final estimate, taken at my grandmother's funeral, was 18 or so, give or take. Only one of the girls was ever widowed, though a few came pretty close.

Throughout my childhood there were always several aunts, along with any number of my cousins, camping out at my grandparents' house, having recently left or been left by some soon-to-be former husband thereafter to be referred to as good ol' Uncle What's-His-Name-Never-Liked-the-Sumbitch-Much-Anyhow.

Consequently, while my cousins and I shared a rather colorful childhood, we also developed a fairly dim view of marriage. Most of us agreed, in fact, that of the half-dozen aunts whose marriages survived more than 10 years, at least three, maybe four, should have gotten out while the getting was good, so to speak.

The exception was our grandparents.

Fred Roberts Wilde and Neta Nellie Hensley fell in love when they were children, married in their late teens and, for more than 50 years, shared a life of romance and adventure.

While their daughters supplied the adventure, the romance

was all their own doing, fueled over time by a passion that could only be explained as a thing.

They had a *thing* for each other.

To see it, you needed only to be in their presence for a few moments, especially when they were having a fight.

For the most part, their disagreements were in theory only, beginning with their saying precisely what they thought of the given situation, and often as not, what they thought of the parties involved.

In the end, whatever differences remained between them, they found themselves on common ground. Much like one person with mixed feelings, it was as if they had no choice but to work it out.

They also did a lot of kissing, especially for old people with false teeth. And more than once, when they didn't know I was watching, I saw them slow dancing together in the kitchen—to music that played only in their minds.

Even then, I always figured, it was the kissing and the dancing that kept them together.

Though the compromising on differences probably didn't hurt.

I was 20 years old when I met him. We dated for six months before he proposed, and two months later, we were married. When he told me that he didn't believe in divorce, I didn't mention that I scarcely believed in marriage. All I knew was that he and I seemed to have a *thing* for each other. And I hoped that somehow, it might last.

Funny, isn't it, how the qualities that people initially find attractive are often the same things that eventually drive them crazy, if not apart?

He was the strong, silent type, which I found incredibly

appealing. And I could talk to anyone about anything, he said, and he liked that a lot in a woman.

Little did we know that strong and silent could also mean stubborn and tight-lipped. As in, definitely not appealing. And talking to anybody about anything could mean never shutting up. As in, really not very likable at all.

There were, of course, other things that attracted us to each other. I liked his car, for example, and he liked my body.

Neither of which held up well, however, over the test of time.

And yet here we are, celebrating the 24th anniversary of a marriage that had little reason to last. I don't pretend to understand it. I've seen better marriages fall apart for a whole lot less, it seems.

But in 25 years, if we are still married, and someone asks me to explain, I'll say:

I learned to like basketball. He learned to do laundry. We had three children who filled our lives with adventure.

And we slow danced in the kitchen and kissed a lot, for old people.

We had a thing for each other, and it lasted. Grace of God. And together, we were better, somehow we were more, than we ever could have been apart.

But you'll have to ask me in 2018.

The Birdbath
- April 12, 1993 -

T he birdbath was a fixture, a not-so-attractive, front-yard centerpiece, when we bought the house more than 20 years ago.

It looked old even then, dingy with age, its bowl tinged green with algae, its base settled into the ground, as if it had been there, and comfortably so, for a very long time. Maybe even, I thought, since 1913, when the house was built, assuming they had such things back then.

No doubt, it had bathed a lot of birds.

I liked thinking about it.

I especially liked thinking about the kind of people who might have put it there—all the families before mine who had called this house "home," who had welcomed friends through its doors, and baked bread in its kitchen, and nursed babies in its bedrooms, and pulled weeds in its yard—years before my husband and I, or even our parents, were born.

What were their lives like? How long were they here? Were they happy? Were they in love? Did they delight in their children? Who planted the azaleas? What kinds of birds came their way?

Funny, isn't it, how something like a birdbath can pose so many questions, conjure up so many images, and yet offer so few answers?

We talked about replacing it, but somehow, we never got around to it. With a house that old, and three babies to boot, we had bigger fish to fry.

So the birdbath remained, standing guard like a sentry, filled with rainwater in winter, or sprinkler water in summer, or with mud when the kids felt creative.

Then one day, I read somewhere that birdbaths must be

cleaned frequently, lest they become breeding grounds for harmful bacteria that could, technically speaking, wipe out every feathered friend in the neighborhood, short of chickens.

I do not believe everything I read. I had my doubts about the dangers of birdbath bacteria. But things that require frequent cleaning tend not to fare well at my house. And I did not wish to risk going down in history as the Woman Who Single-handedly Wiped Out the Entire Bird Population of Pacific Grove.

So the birdbath became a planter. Occasionally, it even held living plants.

Daffodils in spring.

Petunias in summer.

Marigolds in fall.

Stiff, dead stalks in winter.

Actually, stiff dead stalks were my specialty, pretty much the standard crop. But once in a while, the birdbath would bloom, and then it was something to see.

At least, it was until last week, when I broke it.

Never mind how.

Suffice it to say that the older I get, the more my life seems to resemble an "I Love Lucy" skit. If I had a friend named Ethel, I'd be dangerous. But the worst thing about breaking the birdbath was breaking the news to my husband.

"You what?" he said.

"I broke it."

"You broke it?"

"It was an accident."

"You broke it?"

"I broke it and it can't be fixed."

Oops. Wrong thing to say to Mr. Fix-it, who seldom sees anything that can't be fixed. But one look at the pile of rubble lying in the front yard and Mr. Fix-it became Mr. Replace-it.

He spent the last several days of his summer vacation—before heading back to the classroom to gear up for another year of teaching—visiting garden supply shops near and far in search of the perfect birdbath, meaning one that we could afford and not hate.

I suggested that he think of it as an adventure, something that he would look back on one day and laugh. He suggested that I not break the next one.

Finally he found one to his liking and dragged it home to his workshop, where he filled the base with wet cement to make it more difficult for me to tip over and break. Then, before it dried, he carved an inscription in the base and summoned me to come see.

It looked a lot like the old birdbath, I thought, except it was new, of course, and not cracked. And it would do just fine as either a birdbath or planter, something we have yet to decide.

One day years from now, long after we are gone, and another family has taken up residence in our place, someone will tip it over, despite its weighing several tons, and find an inscription on the base, some initials carved within a heart.

If they know nothing else at all about us—we, who lived in this house before they did and raised three children and witnessed so many wonders within its walls—they will, at least, know this:

Once, long ago, in 1993, R.R. loved S.R. enough to set it in cement.

And I suspect they'll like thinking about that.

Very Big Boy

- September 3, 1993 -

Maybe you felt it when you woke up this morning. Something was different, though you weren't sure what or why. Same weather, with fall still weeks away. Same face in the mirror. Same coffee in the cup. Same reasons to get out of bed. But the air this morning was filled with adventure, enough to make old, familiar things seem new.

If you felt it, you weren't alone.

Hundreds of thousands of children in small towns and big cities throughout the country woke up early this morning, sat straight up in their beds, and stared wide-eyed with excitement or terror at the long-awaited First Day of School.

Most of us remember when that day came for us. We recall what we wore, who we sat with, what we ate, even how we felt, though not nearly as intensely.

And for some reason, we laugh at the memory, though we found nothing in the least bit funny about it at the time.

I remember fat chunky crayons and mysterious-looking books and the taste of white paste on my tongue; a boy I loved and a girl I hated, both of them instantly at first sight; and the view from the swings on the playground at recess, when I first saw the world upside down.

My teacher's name was Mrs. Burgess. She was old and smelled like the cod liver oil pills that she handed out and told us to swallow, most of which we squished under the chairs.

She could be tough if you crossed her. But I liked the sound of her voice when she read to us at rest time, and the way she smoothed my hair with her hand whenever she passed by my desk.

I especially liked feeling important—feeling that I had a

purpose. And I decided that next to my grandmother's kitchen, school was the best place to be.

Years later, when my children started school, I recalled all those feelings. And I did all the things they tell you to do so your child will have a positive experience and you won't feel like scum:

1. Arrange for your child to visit his/her classroom and visit his/her teacher prior to the first day of school.
2. Purchase school supplies and a sturdy backpack; label all personal items, especially jackets, with the child's name.
3. Familiarize yourself with the route to be taken to and from school.
4. Talk with your child about his/her feelings; tell the child about your own experience with the first day of school.

Check. I did all that. I also told them not to put much faith in first impressions; keep away from the swings; and never put anything in their mouths that didn't come in their lunchboxes.

And as my first two children toddled happily off to school and returned without incident, I began to think that, unlike *some* parents, I knew what I was doing.

Big mistake. Mother Nature, I learned, prides herself on keeping parents humble.

My third child's approach to school was somewhat different from his siblings'. He had this rag of a blanket he'd grown quite partial to, having dragged it around with him most of his life. And it didn't take a degree in child psychology to see he was banking on dragging it to school.

And so we talked. Yes, he said, he was looking forward to

school. Yes, he knew it was a wonderful place for big, strong, smart, *mature* boys like him. And oh, by the way, he added matter-of-factly, he would be taking his blankie with him, or else they would both be staying at home.

Desperate, I sought professional help.

His father, the high school teacher, told him he might as well give his blankie up now, because most high schools have a policy stating: No Blankies in Lockers or Anywhere Else on Campus at Any Time.

His sister, the second grader, told him not to take it because it was disgusting and she would die of embarrassment.

And his brother, the fifth-grader, told him to leave it at home because he didn't want to have to beat up on all the kids who would call him a wuss.

Miraculously, he seemed to have a change of heart. On the first day of school, he woke early, dressed quickly, ate his Cheerios, brushed his teeth, and announced that he was ready to face the world—without a blanket.

In front of the school, after a quick kiss and a "See ya, Mom," he left me standing alone, choking on the magnificent sight of his blond curls bobbing up the walk.

Then suddenly, he turned and ran back to where I stood, unzipped his new backpack, pulled out his blanket and quickly stuffed it into my arms.

"Somebody might see it," he whispered, grinning sheepishly, "and besides, Mom, you might need it."

"Thanks," I said, "I'd enjoy the company."

Whose Life?

- April 10, 1994 -

Recently my daughter suggested rather strongly that I should get a life. That was her implication, if not her exact words. She later tried to retract it, to soften, but no.

Anything can be forgiven. But there are things, once said, that can't be taken back, words that can't be softened.

I did not take it lightly.

Get a life? I beg your pardon. You can accuse me of all sorts of things, and I'll be the first to admit them. But don't try to tell me I don't have a life. I have more life than I know what to do with.

I've got a full-time job and a family (a husband, three not-yet-grown children and a neurotic dog), a house that defies order, and a yard that should have Agent Orange for a gardener. I even have friends whose names I recall at times.

If I had more of a life I'd be dead.

But we define life differently, my daughter and I. She is 18 and I am, well, old enough to be her mother. We live in the same house, but on different planets.

Still, she's never been unduly critical of my lifestyle, or the lack of it. And I've never had major complaints about hers. Minor, maybe, never major. We've always seemed to share so much in common our differences were merely interesting.

Until lately.

This is the summer of betweens. She's between high school and college; I'm between the asylum and the poorhouse.

Things are supposed to be different—we know it, but neither of us is sure how.

We're still mother and daughter, always have been, always

will be. But the job descriptions, the roles and the rules, are changing.

Frankly, I'm confused.

As far as I can tell, I'm still supposed to support her financially. But I'm not supposed to ask questions about where she's going or when she's coming back.

And I'm supposed to be available when she needs me, say, to iron a blouse or drive her to work. But I'm not to expect her to be available at all, because, hey, she's not my little girl anymore, she has friends, she has a job, she has a life.

I can understand that. I was 18 once, a fact my daughter finds hard to believe even with my senior photo as proof.

In 1966, 18 didn't look the same as it does now, but it felt the same, or close.

I remember it well—the energy, the idealism, the 20-inch waist. The absolute certainty of living forever and never growing old. The frustrating need to be dependent and independent all at once. The pull between family and freedom.

At 18, I thought I knew just about all there was to know, and what I didn't know, I didn't want to be told.

I also thought that if my mother had ever known anything, she had long since forgotten it, due to extreme old age.

She was 40. Talk about needing a life.

I told her I thought she ought to get out more often, do something interesting, have a little fun.

"My life is about as interesting as I can stand," she said. "I work Monday through Friday, clean my house on Saturday, see my mother every Sunday, rain or shine. I don't need fun. I need help."

The summer before I left home for college, she could not be content with her own life, no, she had to keep meddling in mine—asking where was I going, when was I coming back—things I thought I shouldn't have to answer because, hey, I was not her little girl anymore, I had friends, I had a job, I had a life.

Yes, I remember 18.

I suspect what my daughter meant to tell me was not that I should get a life, but that I should get my nose out of hers.

And that's what I intend to do, as soon as I can figure out how to do it. I intend to live my life, and stay out of hers, in hopes that she'll ask me in on occasion.

I don't need a life. I have one, thank you, a full one at that. But I'll always need, always want, to be a part of hers.

I also need to tell my mother I think she's a lot smarter than she used to be. But she still ought to get out more often.

A Middle

—

June 19, 1994 to September 3, 1997

Night Swimming
- June 19, 1994 -

Lately I have spent a lot of time thinking about birds. Babies, too. And fish. I have found in such things a kind of salvation, a refuge I'd not previously known to exist.

I don't pretend to understand it; I don't know how or why it works. But salvation, like the grace that grants it, doesn't need to be understood. It needs only to be enjoyed. You take it as a gift, no questions asked, just being glad you found it.

Recently, when his annual physical turned up a need for major surgery, my husband, ever the jock, vowed to leave the hospital in record time: four days, maybe five, a week tops. But one week became two, then two became three. And somewhere along the way, my mind began to wander perhaps a little too freely and I took up an interest in birds.

They congregated at a feeder outside the window of his hospital room: blue jays and pigeons, doves and quail, woodpeckers and others I couldn't name except to call them Lucy or Fred.

"Look," I'd say, shaking my husband's bed, "those pigeons are back. How can they eat like that and still fly?"

He seldom bothered to answer; just raised an eyebrow and tried to smile. Morphine works wonders with pain, I'm told, but it does little for conversation.

So while he slept, or rather, while he drifted in and out of consciousness, I thought long and hard about birds.

They are, I realized, fascinating creatures, full of purpose, marked by a calling, content to live by instinct. I wondered why I'd not noticed it before.

I also found, by thinking of birds, I didn't have to think of other things: not the maddening hum of the IV pump, or the blinking lights on the monitors, or the tubes and wires that held as hostage the strongest man I'd ever known.

Not the old woman next door chanting "pain, pain, pain," or the teenage girl who'd attempted suicide, or the young man down the hall dying with AIDS.

Not my mother back East, fighting her own battle with cancer. Not my children or my job or my house or my dog. And best of all, I did not have to think about the future. Not if I thought about birds.

But birds tend to disappear around sundown. I don't know where they go, but if they have any nightlife to speak of, they don't spend it at hospital feeders. So after dark, I would think about babies.

Believe it or not, you don't have to be a relative or even a close family friend to visit newborns at the nursery window.

It's as if the babies belonged not just to their families, but to all of us—to you and me and everyone else on the planet— which, in a real sense, they do.

So look all you want, no obligation. You can walk back and forth to see them all, comparing sizes or temperaments or hair. Or you can choose just one to study in detail, lean your head against the glass and lose yourself in wonder. Sort of like window shopping for diamonds. Hospitals owe a huge debt to babies. They ought to deliver them for free.

After visiting hours, when the nursery window closed, I'd start thinking about fish. Not every hospital boasts an indoor fishing pond, but this one did, a fountain under a skylight. It was stocked with what someone called koi, sort of a gold-plated version of catfish, whose apparent purpose in life, other than to eat and swim and maybe mate on occasion, was to be beautiful. And so they were.

The real beauty, of course, in this or any hospital is not its décor, but its people. Take it all away—the fancy fish, the rooms with views, the fabulous art collection—you'd still have the heart, the essence of healing, in doctors and nurses, orderlies and aides, technicians and volunteers. No, they're not gods, we only see them as such when they hold in their hands a life we cherish.

What the fish do is offer diversion.

Sometimes, late at night, when lights were dimmed to lull patients to sleep, I'd imagine slipping out of my husband's room, past the nurse's station, up the stairs and then into the fountain to go swimming by moonlight with fancy fish.

I never did so, mainly for fear I'd get caught and end up on CNN. Given a few more days, I doubt I'd have cared.

But then my husband was sent home at last with orders to take it easy. So now he's standing on a ladder in his Agent Orange outfit trying to trim the ivy. And I am trying to write a column.

Writing is harder to think about than are birds or babies or fish. But I've found in it, too, at times, a kind of salvation.

And I'm hoping to find it there again.

Saving a Spot

- August 21, 1994 -

As a child, I always imagined that the hardest trip to the cemetery to visit the grave of a loved one would be that first time—at the burial—while the memories and the sense of loss were still as fresh as the grave itself.

But I know better now. It's not the first trip that's the hardest, but the second. Or so it was for me.

My parents divorced when I was two, and my mother soon remarried. But my father remained a bachelor, living his last 40 years on the farm where he'd grown up in the mountains of North Carolina.

It was there I knew him best. I lived with my mother, but spent vacations—Christmas, Easter, and summer—with my dad and his parents on the farm.

Rumor had it he was quite popular with the ladies thereabouts—could have had his pick of widows and spinsters. But if he had the slightest interest in any of them, he never let me see it.

In all my memories, he was alone.

Sometimes we took long drives together to no place in particular, bouncing over winding mountain roads with the windows rolled down, breathing air as sweet as creation and singing along with the radio.

He never sang with any seriousness. Not my dad. He was a jokester, always making up silly lyrics just to get me to laugh. He even did it in church.

I remember just one exception, when I was 10 years old. We'd been riding along for about an hour, singing and laughing, when the radio faded out on us and we decided to give it a rest.

Dad drove in silence, eyes fixed on the road ahead, with one hand on the wheel and the other dangling a cigarette out the window. Then he started to sing.

It was a song and a voice I'd not heard before, nor would I ever hear them again, except in memory. The melody was pure country —low and sweet and filled with longing—and the words went something like this: "I'm all dressed up with no place to go..."

Had he not stopped—to take a drag on his cigarette and let the smoke out with a laugh—I'm not sure how I'd have stood it. Fathers are not supposed to be lonely. We both knew it. And he never let me see him lonely again, not even years later, in the veterans' hospital, when I visited him after his stroke.

Three years ago, at his funeral, my sister and I took refuge in the small gathering of family and friends who came to pay their respects. They rocked us like babies in their arms, they soothed us with kind words and simple food and lavishly embellished stories about the time he did this or the day he pulled that. And they stood by us, shoulder to shoulder, as we buried him.

It was a perfect October day, crisp and clear, with fall ablaze on the mountains around us—the sort of day he loved best. Strange as it may sound, it was not hard to be there, surrounded as we were, by beauty and loving-kindness.

The hard time came a year later, on my first visit home after the funeral. By then, his gravestone was in place and my sister suggested we go see it together. I'm not much for visiting cemeteries. I figure, what's the point of a visit, if nobody's home? But I couldn't let my sister go alone.

The cemetery of the little country church was divided loosely into family plots—Smiths here, Cases there, Wilsons up on the ridge. Finding the grave was easy. Seeing it was not.

There was a permanence to it I'd not felt at the funeral. His name and his dates of birth and death were now set, undeniably, in stone. And the wound in the earth had healed without a scar, as if it had always held him. My sister gripped my hand so hard it hurt.

Then we noticed it—another new marker right next to Dad's. It belonged to a woman about his age, who was still very much alive. Her family plot lay just up the hill. Yet apparently she had chosen to reserve herself a spot to spend eternity alongside our father.

And suddenly, we smiled—all right, we laughed long and hard, loud enough to wake the dead—set free by the thought that maybe, just maybe, Dad had not been quite as lonely as we had feared.

Songs 4 Mom
- October 10, 1994 -

When my firstborn left home for college some years ago, I wanted to make the leaving easier for him than my mother had made mine for me.

I'm not above using guilt, but unlike my mother, I prefer to save it for the finale rather than the opener. So I tried not to show how hard it was for me to let the boy go, or how much I really missed him. Honest. I was good.

My friends and family were amazed at how easily I shifted mothering gears from hands-on to long-distance.

"Don't you miss him?" they'd ask, studying my face.

"Sure," I'd say, looking away, "but hey, life goes on. He's happy.

I'm happy. I can hardly wait to turn his room into an office..."

I fooled everyone, it seemed, even myself, at times. But I did not fool the boy.

The first time he came home for a weekend—looking older and bigger, and dragging a carload of rancid laundry—I didn't see much of him. He slept late, played hoops with his dad at the gym, went out at night with his friends.

Just like old times.

But Sunday afternoon, as he was packing to go back to school (stuffing the laundry I'd washed and folded for him into a duffel bag) he suddenly remembered something. Fishing in his backpack, he pulled out a small plastic case.

"Here," he said, grinning like the boy who brought me seashells from the beach and pinecones from the forest. "I made this for you."

"What is it?" I laughed, expecting a punchline.

"It's a cassette," he said, hoisting the duffel bag on his big shoulder. "I taped it from a bunch of different albums, some oldies I knew you liked a lot, plus some new stuff you'll like, too."

"You think so?"

"I know so," he said, grinning again. "I know you. You're my mom."

Ten minutes and a long hug later, he was gone, headed back to his future. And I was alone in my room, listening to "Songs 4 Mom."

It was the broadest, oddest mix of music I'd ever heard, or ever cared to hear—27 recordings by 14 artists, some I knew well (Paul Simon, Elton John); some I sort of knew (Eric Clapton, Pink Floyd); and some I'd never heard of (Steel Pulse?).

There were remakes of oldies I'd sung to him when he was a baby (Marvin Gaye's "Mercy, Mercy, Me" by Robert Palmer; Otis

Redding's "Try a Little Tenderness" by The Commitments; and Sonny and Cher's "I Got You, Babe" by The Pretenders).

And there was "new stuff" I'd not heard before, but liked, as he'd predicted (Lynrd Skynrd's "Simple Man"; Robert Palmer's "Housework"; and Peter Gabriel's amazing "It's Accomplished").

I've played that tape countless times, and every time I'm surprised at how much it moves me—not just the music, or that he gave it to me, but that he knew me so well. Well enough to know what I would like before I knew it myself.

Funny, isn't it? All those years, I wasn't sure the boy was listening.

I miss him still. I always will. But it's easier to let someone go, I think, when you know he carries you with him.

Throwing Stones
- November 2, 1994 -

I got in big trouble with my mother for going to the Rolling Stones concert. No, I don't mean 30 years ago when I was a teenager. I mean last week, when I was a middle-aged woman and, according to her, should have had better sense. She seemed particularly galled by the fact that I also took my husband and our college-age children.

"Whatever possessed you to expose them to such corruption?" she asked.

"I don't know," I said. "Whatever possessed you to chew tobacco?"

That is my stopper question. I use it whenever I feel the need to change directions in my mother's train of thought. It derails her every time.

"I don't do that any more," she snapped, "it costs too much. Besides, it's nasty. So, uh, how's your weather?"

The weather was fine at the Oakland Coliseum the night we saw the Stones, a cool, clear October evening, perfect for the World Series. Too bad there's a baseball strike. The grass on the A's infield never looked better. I guess it's easier to keep it in good shape when they've got nobody playing on it.

Our seats were in the lower deck between home plate and first base. We watched the concert in two ways at once—up close on a giant video screen, and far off on the stage out in center field where the Stones looked more like sticks. It occurred to me the whole thing could have been faked and folks wouldn't have had a clue.

Even if they knew, I doubt they'd have cared. They were too busy having a good time.

Especially in our section. Never before, outside of carnival tents and newspaper conventions, have I seen such a fun-loving crosssection of humanity. Two rows down from us sat a bunch of large, burly tattooed men—either Hell's Angels or Hell's Angels wanna-bes—who were celebrating some sort of reunion.

Behind them, and directly in front of our faces, were the backsides of half a dozen teenagers, who stood for the entire performance.

To our left was a rather affectionate group of young couples, whose pairings seemed to change with some regularity. I wasn't sure just who was with whom, until one poor fellow got sick and threw up. I assumed the young woman who used her sweater to clean him up was probably going to be his woman for life.

To our right was a stocky silver-haired woman wearing

bifocals, a hunting vest, and sensible shoes, who clapped off beat and sang the words to every song right along with Mick. And behind us sat a row of quiet, nondescript, fairly forgettable individuals, save for one: a middle-aged man with an inordinate amount of body hair, who removed his shirt and danced half-naked, with his belly swinging side to side and butting me in the back of my head.

I do like to see folks having a good time, don't you? I love being in a big crowd with all sorts of interesting-looking people all laughing and clapping and singing along to the music.

I especially like it if they stay friendly and don't try to beat me up. And you couldn't have asked for a much friendlier crowd than this.

But that is not why I went.

I went to see the Stones.

I went to recall "Beast of Burden" and "Satisfaction" and "Jumpin' Jack Flash," among other memories.

I went to see miracles, like Keith Richards, still living. Who'd have believed it? Mick Jagger, still ugly, sounding better than ever, holding a stadium full of people, young and old alike, captive in the palm of his hand.

I went because I wanted my children to see their parents, not just as Mom and Dad, but as people who were young once—who listened to music with the volume full blast and didn't care what the neighbors thought—and who still like to get down on occasion.

And maybe I went because I knew how much it would gall my mother.

But mostly I went for the music.

Like the song says, I know it's only rock 'n' roll. But I like it.

Keeping Score
- January 25, 1995 -

Some years ago I made my peace with the gym at Monterey High School. Rare is the woman who can call herself a friend of her husband's mistress.

I knew what I was getting into when I married Mr. Wizard, a science teacher, complete with a pocket protector for pens. He said he wanted to coach basketball, to teach character on the court as well as in the classroom. He loved the game almost as much as he loved physics and chemistry and me.

"Fine," I said, "I'll keep score for your games."

So I did, three seasons. Then I had a baby. Three babies in five years. And pretty soon I quit going to games and the only score I kept was how much he was gone and how few assists he had.

"Get used to it," I told myself, "he was a coach when you married him."

But you can know how something works in theory without knowing how it feels in practice. I understood it fine. But I did not like it much at all.

Things changed 12 years ago, when Mr. Wizard moved up to head coach. It meant more responsibility, more time away from home, not a lot more pay. And yet, I wanted him to do it. Not just because he loved it, but because he was good at it. At least I thought so.

He was good at being honest and hardworking and caring—things players ought to see in a coach while learning how to dribble, pass, and shoot; how to be fierce on defense, wise with shots; how to keep your mind on the game if your mom's on drugs or your dad's gone or your girlfriend just broke up with you; how to keep your shorts up and your jersey tucked in.

Important things like that. I wanted him to coach. But I did not want to pay for it with my marriage.

"All right," I said, "count me in. But I'm not keeping score."

After that, I didn't miss many games, home or away. I got there somehow, dragging my children with me.

"Come on, kids," I'd say, luring them into the van, "let's go eat junk food and watch Daddy get beat."

In time, I grew fond of The Pit. That's what they called her, an old, barnlike gym, loud and hot, with an out-of-bounds line that eats up opponents, makes 'em think they're playing in hell.

I used to think she was tacky—the splintered bleachers, avocado paint, a scoreboard nobody over 30 can read.

Now I think she has character. Like the hole my husband cut in the wall to set up a video camera. Or how you have to go upstairs, climb down bleachers, and cross the court to get good seats. Or how, if you sit behind the bench, you have to turn sideways, so your knees don't poke the kids in the back.

Character. She's loaded with it. And she calls it out in the players.

Sometimes, when you think a game is lost, you see it shining suddenly in some young, sweaty face—a stubborn, chin-up look of resolve, a refusal of defeat. Doesn't mean they'll win the game, but it's a victory in itself.

That's why Mr. Wizard decided to coach again this year, even though he's having chemotherapy for cancer.

To him, it's a matter of character.

When you love doing something, when you're good at it, when the people who love you want you to do it, you get that same stubborn look on your face and try not to let anything take it away.

I saw that look Friday night, not just on the faces of my husband and his players, but on their opponents' faces, as well. It was basketball at its best, a showdown: two veteran coaches, two fine teams, both unbeaten in league.

Finally, Salinas, the only undefeated team in California, seemed assured of victory. But Mark Anderson, bless his little shaved head, edged a player onto The Pit's out-of-bounds line, and Monterey won in overtime.

Afterward, my husband credited his players for the victory. (That's the rule: win, it's the kids; lose, it's the coach.) He also gave credit to The Pit.

But when the scorebook was tallied and the lights were dimmed, I was the one he took out to dinner.

Love at First Sound
- February 1, 1995 -

My brother pulled a fast one on the family recently. Had we known what he was up to, we'd have tried to talk some sense into him. Which is probably why he didn't bother to tell us he was planning to run off and get married.

He always was a stubborn little cuss, even before he went to the state school for the deaf and the blind.

The school made him stronger, meaner, maybe. But it was always Joe's nature, even as a baby, to take, as they say, nothing from nobody, to find his own way in the world, darkness be damned.

When he was little, four or five, he liked to get up for the sunrise, and nothing we could say or do could make him stay in bed. I watched him sometimes, feeling his way to the kitchen window where he'd sit, head bowed, waiting for the sun.

When it rose, he couldn't see it, of course, but he could feel its warmth through the window. Then he'd turn his face directly toward it, grinning, until he couldn't take the heat anymore.

Occasionally, he'd make me get up and tell him what the sunrise looked like. If I got it wrong, he'd say, "Nope, that's not it, try again."

So I had to keep trying until he'd say, "That sounds about right to me."

He was equally stubborn with fear, never letting it get the upper hand. He'd push his tricycle into ditches, beat up the deaf boys who teased him, stand his ground with any monster, any suffering, real or imagined.

Take the way he played with caps.

Normal children loaded them into cap pistols, held them a safe distance away and shot them at their neighbors.

Not Joe. Pistols were a waste of time, he said. He preferred a hammer. He'd unwind a roll of caps on a big, flat rock, then hammer away, pop, pop, pop, until they were all gone.

If he missed, as he often did, and bloodied a finger, he'd let out an impressive stream of obscenities, after which my mother would take his caps and make him come inside.

But sometimes Joe would hit just right to launch an explosion loud as thunder that echoed on the mountains. He'd sit, cocking an ear to catch the last faint pop. Then he'd throw back his head and laugh with abandon—with what struck me as the joy of being alive.

I called it his cap-busting laugh.

My mother called it contrariness.

It was a birthmark, she said, like his blindness. She was never sure what caused either condition, but she carried them, like stones, around her neck.

Guilt isn't picky. Right or wrong, it will gladly ride any willing host.

We were all willing—my mother, my stepfather, my sister, brother and I. We wore Joe's blindness like a family coat of arms, rallied around him, fought to protect him, dared anyone to laugh at him or harm him in any way—even after he grew up and moved out on his own, a man, free and clear of us at last.

Twenty years later, he still says we're nosy, bossy, overly protective.

I say, what are families for? It's surely no reason to run off and get married without bringing what's-her-name home to Sunday dinner.

"So what's she like," I ask when he finally answers his phone.

"She's great," he says, "you'll like her. Three weeks isn't long to know a person. But I've been waiting for Tommie Jean all my life."

They have much in common, he says, both 43, born the same year, premies in incubators, blinded by too much oxygen. They both play music and sing.

I hear a voice, soft and low, in the background, telling him what to say.

"She says come see us, we'll be glad to have you," he tells me. Then he laughs his cold, cap-busting laugh.

It's a sound I've missed for too many years and suddenly, perhaps forever, I am in Tommie Jean's debt.

So. My brother's married, taking orders, no less. He says "we" instead of "I," and turns his face toward the warmth of a voice where, for him, the sun now rises and sets.

And somehow that sounds about right to me. Like Joe says, even a blind man can fall in love at first sight.

The Dress

- August 27, 1995 -

On the occasion of her 70th birthday—surrounded by a houseful of family and friends—my mother, in a rare display of decorum, decided to give a little speech.

Rising with great effort from her bed, she pulled on a bathrobe, poufed up her perm, popped in her dentures, and shuffled with purpose out to the living room where the party was just winding down.

"Well," she said, catching her breath and waiting for the crowd to quiet, "I'm glad we could all be together today. I hope you all live to be as old as I am, and that none of you ever gets cancer. And if I don't see you again on this earth, I'll look for you in heaven."

Turning to go back to bed, she suddenly remembered her manners.

"Thanks for all the food you brought, even though it made me sick," she said, rolling her eyes at my cousin. "Honey, what the hell did you put in that salad?"

When the laughter died, she grinned, pleased with herself that she could still work a crowd.

"And thanks for all the cards and gifts. I loved them all, even though," she said, rolling her eyes this time at me, "what I really wanted was..."

"Don't say it," I warned her, "if I hear it again, I swear I'm packing up and going home."

One day last spring, I was out shopping for a pair of sensible shoes (the kind that look dorky but don't kill your feet) when suddenly I heard this voice—low and sultry; sounded just like Antonio Banderas—telling me to forget that sensible nonsense and buy myself something *youngggg!*

Next thing you know, I'm walking out of the store wearing this cute little ankle-length, blue denim jumper with slits up the sides all the way to HERE—know what I mean?

I wish you could see it.

It's the kind of thing my 20-year-old daughter might be willing to wear, if it came in a size 3, and her thighs were real tanned.

I swear I don't know what came over me. Spring fever, maybe? The hysterectomy I'd just had? The fact that it was on sale? Who knows?

For whatever reason, I bought it. And I wear it, God help me, at least twice a week. It's a lot like wearing sensible shoes. Looks dorky, maybe, but it feels real good. And it never hurts my feet.

Anyhow, when I flew home last month for my mother's birthday, I wore that jumper on the flight.

I expected to be greeted with a well-intentioned lecture on the value of acting and dressing one's age and "not giving people nothing to talk about, because God knows, people love to talk."

But instead, before she even hugged my neck, my mother took a look at what I was wearing and said, "I want one just like it."

She had to be joking, right? I mean, a woman her age in something like that? What would people say?

"For my birthday," she said, "that's what I want."

"Mother," I told her, "be sensible. You're eight inches shorter than I am. On you, this thing would drag the ground like a bridal train."

"They make petites," she said.

I knew I'd never hear the end of it. When I got back to California, I went shopping. In the petites. And I found a denim jumper. Long, but not as long as mine. With no unseemly slits up the sides.

Then I wrapped it up, mailed it off, and waited for her to call.
"I love it!" she gushed. "I might even wear it to church."
"Swell," I said. "Does it drag on the ground when you walk?"
"It's a tad long," she said, "but it can be altered. They'll whack off a few inches, hem it good as new...then I'll have them put some slits up the sides."

One Way Home
- December 20, 1995 -

Three weeks before Christmas, my sister called to say our mother's three-year battle with cancer had reached its final hours.

"Hurry," she said, and I did. I booked a reservation on the next available flight, then made a dozen calls to clear my calendar of things that had been planned for months—speaking engagements, jury duty, and Christmas—all changed by one word: "Hurry."

My flight landed just before midnight. It was the first time in 30 years that I'd been home in December. I'd forgotten how cold a Carolina Christmas can be.

I rented a car, drove to the hospital, slipped in through the ER and somehow found my mother's room. Truthfully, I had my doubts about her condition. The woman is a notorious actress. She got it from her mother, who was known more than once to summon us all to her bedside by feigning a stroke.

I was hoping that my mother—who'd sounded fine on the

phone a few days ago—had faked this "turn for the worse" to get me home for Christmas. I expected as I walked in her room to see her light up and laugh at what she'd pulled. I was all set to play the fool.

Why is it when the inevitable, the long-dreaded finally comes, we find it so hard to believe?

One knowing look, one frail hug, and I knew my mother wasn't acting. I'd never seen her as serious, as forthright about anything, as she was now about dying.

"You're here," she said.

"I'm here," I said, "and I'm not leaving."

"I want to go home," she said.

"Can't take you home tonight," I said, "maybe tomorrow."

The last time we'd talked, I had promised her if she'd be patient until after the holidays, I'd fly home in January, check her out of the hospital and take care of her at home for a while. She never was much for patience.

"I'm going home," she said, her eyes flashing. "I'm going soon and you won't have to take me."

Over the next three days, my mother stood her ground, fought like a soldier—no, like a mother—to buy time to say her goodbyes.

One by one, they came: Her sisters. Her nieces and nephews. The grandchildren she raised as her own. Her blind child, a man now, and still her greatest worry. My sister, her nurse. My stepfather, her husband for 43 years. And finally, my brother, her baby, estranged for too many years.

They all came and went and came again. And between the visits, early morning, late at night, I stayed by her side and tried to think of what I was supposed to do. I like to know what's expected of me, and this time, I hadn't a clue.

I brushed her hair, powdered her neck, washed her face with a cool cloth. I told her stories about her grandchildren, recalled good times when I was small. I read to her from the Bible. Even sang when no one was listening. I don't know if it helped her, but it helped me.

Then one morning when my sister sent me out with orders to "get a shower or else," my mother took her last breath and went home.

Two days later, we laid her to rest alongside her parents, her brother, and six of her sisters. Then we went back to her house, some 50 of us strong, to eat ham and potato salad and sweet pies prepared in her honor by the good women from her church.

That night, as I drove my brother to his apartment, I fell into an old habit, describing for him things he couldn't see: the Christmas lights on Main Street, decorations in the windows, green wreaths on the doors of the church.

He listened hard to contain it, to see all that beauty in his mind.

"Mama always wanted to get you home for Christmas," he said.

"I know," I said. "It's lovely. I'll take it as her gift."

Held Up Again
- January 7, 1996 -

My mother hated being late. She hated it so much, in fact, that she was never late for anything. At least, that's how she saw it.

Other people were late; she was just "held up." Not by the gun, but by some unforeseen circumstance beyond her control. Usually, she blamed it on her children.

I remember Sunday mornings, how she would march about, cracking a bullwhip of words above our heads, "Eat! Put your shoes on! Stop twisting his ears! You're going to make us late for church again!"

An hour later, we'd be sitting in the car waiting for her to get the curlers out of her hair. But if she was late, it was because we held her up. She swore some day we'd make her late to her own funeral.

There's an old Southern saying that when a women dies, good or bad, she's reborn in her daughter. When I went home to bury my mother, I picked up where she left off, cracking that same whip to keep everybody moving.

But people in my family flat-out refuse to hurry. The house could be in flames, dropping cinder, and my sister would have to finish her make-up. My stepfather would have to grab some coffee. And my brother would have to do whatever he sets his mind on, because that is the only thing Joe ever does.

"Strong-willed," my mother called him. It's what he had to be, she said, to survive being born blind. To grow up to be independent. To stand on his own, a man.

Me, I just called him stubborn. But I backed him up some months ago when he married Tommie Jean after knowing her three weeks. Like him, she'd been blind all her life, he said, but she was his wife now, whether we liked it or not.

Mother didn't like it a bit. But despite what some said, it did not cause her death. What killed her was cigarettes, not heartache.

The day of her funeral, I tried to keep busy. It's what I do, how I cope in a crisis. I keep moving real fast until it's over, then I do the dishes and fall apart.

But my brother and his wife kept slowing me down. First, Joe made me take him to the funeral home to see if the casket my sister and I had chosen would be "suitable."

What he really wanted, I soon realized, was simply to see it— to know what a casket "looked like," how it felt, how it smelled.

"Here's where her head will go," I said, guiding his hand, "and here's how the lid will close. But remember, it isn't for her. It's only for her body."

"I know," he said, "it's real nice. Mama would be pleased."

Next , Tommie Jean wanted me to show her the flowers. All of them.

"Those are lilies," I said, brushing pollen off her nose, "and these are roses and carnations."

"They're all pretty," she said smiling, "but I like roses best."

"Mother did, too," I said.

Then, while I was trying to get everybody dressed for the funeral, Joe and my sister got in a fight when he refused to wear a tie.

"It'll kill Mama," my sister said, "if you don't wear a tie."

"No, it won't," Joe snapped, "Mama knows how I hate ties."

"Don't worry," Tommie Jean told me, "I'll talk him into it."

And so she did, God bless her. I guess it's why I didn't mind her making us late for the funeral.

We were all set. My sister had her makeup on. My stepfather had his coffee. Joe was in a tie, and we were headed for the door.

"Sister," said Tommie Jean, "do you have time to do my makeup? I want to look pretty today."

For a moment, the clock on the mantel stopped ticking as I studied my sister-in-law's shining face and saw for the first time a beauty.

"No hurry," I said, laughing, recalling Mama's prediction about her funeral. She wouldn't mind if it started a bit late. She'd just say that we had held her up again.

I Wish He Could Be Little, Me Big
- January 15, 1996 -

The only thing I had against him, really, was that he married my mother. And you could hardly blame him for that. Not that she was any catch.

But when my mother set her mind on doing something—say, to marry my father when she was 15, or to leave him when I was two, or to remarry three years later just to spite her mother—she did it. And she left little room for argument. My stepfather, God bless him, never knew what hit him. He had two strikes against him before he ever got to bat.

First, he walked into my life, uninvited, unannounced, unwelcome, and unwanted when I was five years old and quite in love with my daddy.

And second, he was the biggest man I had ever seen. From his flattop haircut all the way down to the soles of his size 13 feet. Big and loud—or he could be. Nothing, it seems, cranks up the volume like a few quick shots of moonshine.

The biggest thing about him was his heart. He would never willingly harm a soul, least of all that of a child. But I didn't know that when I was five, and that made all the difference.

I remember once, driving home one night on a winding mountain road, with my mother asleep in the front seat and my stepfather at the wheel. I didn't the like the way he was driving and I didn't mind telling him so.

"Ten years from now," he said, "when you're old enough to get a license, you can tell me how to drive. For now, why don't you just go to sleep?"

So I did. When I woke up, we were home, he was carrying me into the house and my mother was warning him not to drop me. My face was scrunched against the pocket of his shirt, crumpling the wrapper on his last pack of Camels. I could smell the tobacco and hear the solid beat of his heart. And all I can tell you is what I remember to this day—that I had never felt safer in my life.

After that, whenever we were out late at night, if I was not sound asleep by the time we got home, I would pretend to be.

Why is it sometimes the best people in our lives are like the best lessons—ones we didn't always want to know? I remember a lot about my stepfather. How he found me when I got lost in a snowstorm. How he let my children shoot bottle rockets off his porch on the Fourth of July. How he leaned on my arm and cried like a baby leaving the church after my mother's funeral.

But I don't ever remember him being afraid.

I'm not saying he's afraid now, I just suspect he might be. Age and infirmity and all they entail are enough to put the fear of God in even the bravest soul.

Seems it's time to sell the place he's called home most of his life—the house he and my mother worked so hard to pay for. He needs less space to heat and cool, but mostly he needs people to talk to. So he's ready to consider, at least, moving to a retirement community.

"I'll tell you the truth," he says when I call, "it won't be easy for me to leave this place."

I believe him.

I wish, for just one night, he could be little and I could be big. I would fly across country in a big jumbo jet and slip into the house while he was sound asleep. Then I'd pick him up like a baby in my arms and carry him to the new place across town. And when he woke up, he would see my face and know that he was home and he wouldn't have to be afraid.

But when we can't do what we want to do, we do the best we can. So I tell him it's late and he should go on to bed. And I promise to bring his grandchildren to see him again soon.

Unbreakable

- January 28, 1996 -

We had gone to the mountains to spend a few days in the snow, my husband and I, and of course, our three children, who look grown, but don't always act like it.

It's what we do every winter, get away for a little triathlon competition to see who can win the most arguments, dirty the most dishes, and monopolize the most time in the bathroom. Two days into it, I was ready for a break.

I did not want to spend another day watching my children ski or snowboard or otherwise maim their bodies. I wanted to be left alone.

"Yes, that's right," I told my husband, "I want to sit by this fire, read this book, and sulk."

And so I did. For a while.

But after the kids hit the slopes, he played his ace. Offered to buy me breakfast. It works every time.

I don't know about you, but for me, pancakes are the next best thing to Prozac. Perked me right up. Pancakes and guilt. That is how he got me to go innertubing.

"It'll be fun," he said, as he paid 10 bucks to rent what looked like two giant rubber bagels.

"You go first," I said.

He tightened the strap on his "Grumpy Old Men" hat, hunkered down in his innertube, and gave me a big grin. Then he was off—flying, spinning, bouncing like a top over 175 snow-covered yards. He stopped inches shy of a highway and sat stock-still for a moment. I was sure he'd had a heart attack until he jumped up and waved for me to follow.

If I die, I thought, *it'll make a good obit.*

Then I took a deep breath, closed my eyes and launched myself over the edge.

Halfway down the hill, I had a revelation. I was bobbing along, flopping like a rag doll, trying desperately to get some control. I grabbed at passing trees, tried to steer with my body, dug my heels in the snow, but no. The harder I fought, the faster I flew.

Suddenly it seemed strangely familiar—as if I'd been on that innertube, sliding down that hill, hurtling through space for a very long time. Much like the last year of my life, when I'd seen time and again just how little control I had over my life, let alone the lives of those I loved.

Couldn't stop my husband's illness. Couldn't prevent my mother's death. Couldn't keep my children from growing up.

It's hard work, tedious and exhausting—isn't it?—trying to control the uncontrollable.

What I felt on that hill was not fear, but fatigue. I was bone tired.

So I simply let go. It was not easy to do, but I did it. Just opened my eyes, felt the wind in my hair, leaned back and enjoyed the ride. My husband was impressed.

I'd forgotten how good it feels to live with abandon—to live in the present without fearing the future, without longing for the past. I won't forget it soon.

I went up that hill and down a dozen times, until my legs were shot. Then I sat in my innertube and chucked snowballs at my husband as he whizzed by, ducking and grinning like a little boy.

Once, I even managed to flip him. It was hilarious.

I couldn't wait to get back and tell the kids. I knew they'd be proud.

Pieces of My Heart
- May 1, 1996 -

Sometimes I find a note I left myself, like "RSVP to M.F. ASAP!" But I have no clue as to what it means.

Who the heck was M.F.? What on earth did M.F. want? Did I want to do it? Was I too late? And, if so, was M.F. still speaking to me?

I hate finding notes like that. Sometimes I figure them out. Sometimes I don't. I just hope M.F. is A-OK and doesn't work for the IRS.

Last week, I found a note—three notes, actually—that I left years ago in an old chest where I store keepsakes.

They were written, not by me, but by my children, at different times and ages in their lives. It was no mystery that I kept them; that chest—along with the attic, the garage and every corner of the house—is stuffed with the remnants of three children who are now all but grown and gone.

What puzzled me was why—of all the school reports, Christmas lists and Mother's Day cards I saved—I had chosen to clip these three scraps of paper together, to set them apart from the rest? As if they belonged together. As if they formed a pattern, a whole I'd seen, but forgotten.

I'll start with the oldest. One day, 20 years ago, I found in the mailbox a "letter," posted with an S&H green stamp. Written in crayon, its message was simple: two hearts signed simply, "JOSH." Good thing I saved it. It was the only letter he'd ever write that didn't ask for money.

The second note came from my daughter when she was eight, that sweet age that seems to shine like the sun before the storm of adolescence.

"Dear Mom," she wrote, in careful cursive, if faulty spelling, "I love you very much. You're a very kind woman and a very butiful woman to. I thank god for you very much. Love, Joanna."

I don't recall why she wrote it. She's written stacks of such notes over the years, most of which I've kept. It seems that, like her mother, she finds it easier to write, rather than to say, how she feels.

The third note, like my third child, was different from the first two. He wrote it when he was seven, after he noticed that I always winked when I talked about the Easter Bunny or Santa or how we didn't need to stop and ask for directions because Daddy really knew how to get there.

"Dear tooth fairie," he wrote, "Two teeth came out of my mouth but I lost one! Please give me double-credit! Your friend, Nate."

I remember how proud, how pleased with himself he seemed as he handed me that note, and the bloody tooth that went with it. How he grinned like a jack-o'-lantern and winked.

So there they were, three notes, each different, all treasures, much like the children who wrote them. I decided to frame them, along with a snapshot of the authors, at ages one to five, laughing and holding onto each other as if they would never let go.

I bought a frame and began making a collage, overlapping and shaping their notes, just as I had their childhoods.

It was then I saw it, the reason why I had saved them as one all these years. Pieced together just so, into a ragged little puzzle, they formed the exact shape of my heart.

Ordinary People
- May 5, 1996 -

For days now, I've been pulling for Alex to get out of here and get on with her young life.

A 16-year-old girl has better things to do than to lie around in a hospital, hooked up to gross machines.

I remember her eyes, glazed with fever, wide with fear, the night they rolled her in the room and parked her bed near my husband's.

He'd been there for a week already—in the intensive care unit of Stanford Medical Center in Palo Alto—fighting complications from surgery.

I don't know what Alex is fighting. I haven't asked. It's enough to know she is fighting for her life.

That is what ICU is, of course, a place where people, young and old, fight to stay alive. I knew that before, but I know it differently now. Lately, it seems, I think of little else.

Visits in ICU are brief, the first 10 minutes on the hour; for family members only, two at a time. We take turns, my children and I, when they drive up to see their dad. Usually, I'm his only visitor.

If I keep out of the way and don't ask stupid questions, the nurses let me stay longer than 10 minutes. They say my husband is calmer, sleeps better, when I'm near. I believe it. After 27 years of marriage, you get good at putting each other to sleep.

Dogs, I'm told, have much the same effect on their masters. But pets aren't allowed in ICU, so I stay as long as I can—too long, at times, yet never long enough. As hard as it is to visit, it is harder by far to leave.

That seems especially true for Alex's parents. Her dad arrives early to brush the tangles from her hair. Her mom stays late to read her stories and rub her legs.

They have the look parents get when a child is at risk and there's nothing to do but to wait and be champions of hope. They're like porcelain dolls with painted smiles; cheery, but ready to break.

In the rare moments when I am not entirely consumed by concern for my husband, I feel my heart reach out to them, silently, prayerfully, lifting them up. I suspect they do the same for me.

Life is hard in the ICU—confusing, exhausting, scary. That is how one nurse described it. Imagine what it's like for the patients.

Never dark, never quiet, no sense of day or night. All those tubes and monitors, all that beeping and blinking. It's like being a prisoner in a video arcade, without quarters to play the games.

The level of care is wonderful. You wouldn't want it any less. But it's seldom without side effects.

One morning, after yet another long and restless night, my husband began to show signs of strain.

"You know Melba?" he asked.

An elderly patient in a nearby bed, Melba had refused to wake up after surgery despite loud and endless pleas from her family and nurses that she at least try to wiggle her toes.

"I know Melba," I answered. "How's she doing?"

"I don't know," snapped my husband. "I just wish she'd wake up and wiggle her damn toes."

It was not one of his better days in the ICU. Nor was it his worst.

But today is a good day, best day so far in the two weeks since his surgery. Because this morning, he's been transferred from the ICU to a normal room where he can sleep like a baby until 5 A.M., when the vampires come to draw his blood.

And because Alex, who's just had a shampoo and looks fabulous, will be out of her, too, by noon.

And because last night—after everybody quit nagging her about it—Melba, God bless her, woke up and wiggled her toes.

Morning Glories
- September 29, 1996 -

I was sitting at my desk, working in theory, daydreaming in fact, when I saw something creeping over my back fence. Morning glories. My neighbor must have planted them months ago. And now, here they were, spilling into my yard, climbing into my memory.

My grandfather loved to garden. He found joy both in what he grew and in the growing.

"Look," he'd say, his face lighting up at the latest bloom, "Solomon in all his glory was not so arrayed."

That's how he talked, mixing metaphors, peppering quotes from the King James with personal observations, to illustrate his point, whatever that might be.

Some people—including his wife, nine daughters and various members of the churches where he sometimes preached on Sunday mornings—found him hard to figure.

Not me. I listened to his words and watched his eyes, and together, they made perfect sense. We understood each other, my granddad and I, in the way old people and children often do.

Of all the flowers in his garden, he was especially fond of two. Best of all, he loved the rose of Sharon, a tall shrub with stick-like limbs and ruffled pink blooms. It was also the name that he used for me. "Rose of Sharon," he would say, giving me a wink and patting my head, "the most beautiful flower in all the Holy Land."

I never saw the Holy Land, but every time my granddad called me rose of Sharon, I would bloom like a rose in the desert.

His second favorite flower was the morning glory. He planted them every year and let them wander where they pleased, snaking over fences, swirling around trees. He called them trumpets of the Lord because, he said, they shouted the glory of God.

"Can you hear them?" he would ask and I would nod and say, "Yes, sir, I hear them loud and clear." Then we would have ourselves a big laugh.

When I was five, my mother decided to run off and get married again. The night she left, when I finally figured out what she was up to, I pitched an impressive fit. Even my grandparents, who were usually a sure source of comfort, found me inconsolable.

The next morning, after my grandmother made my favorite breakfast (biscuits and oatmeal, hold the raisins), my grandfather took me out to the garden. The morning glories were just waking up, stretching and tilting their lovely blue trumpets slowly toward the sun. As he lifted me up to pinch a few spent blooms off the vines, he whispered in my ear a verse from Psalms: "Weeping may endure for a night, but joy cometh in the morning."

I had heard that verse in Sunday School. I almost knew it by heart. But that morning, stuffed with my grandmother's biscuits, sheltered in the safety of my grandfather's arms and surrounded by so much glory, I began to understand it, to claim it as my own.

That was the memory that climbed my fence last week, a gift from my neighbor's yard. Yesterday I went out and bought myself two pots of morning glories and set them on a bench outside my kitchen window. Yes, I know, it's late. They'll be gone soon.

But they are here today—I heard them this morning, loud and clear, trumpets of God shouting for joy—and who is to say about tomorrow?

Joy, it seems, is hard to find these days. I'm learning to find it one morning at a time.

Coach Randall's 27-Year Career
- November 5, 1996 -

The new coach asked me to write something about the old coach, my husband, Randy, who retired this season.

"Like what?" I asked.

"Like your memories of him as a coach," he said, "you know, like what you do to him in your column all the time."

"You mean, use him and basketball metaphorically to explore the meaning of life?"

"Uh, sure. Whatever."

My husband's 27 years in coaching were my years too, and our children's. Good or bad, they shaped our family: good mainly, but there were times that did not feel good at all. Most families have a trademark, a blessing and a curse. The Kennedy's had politics. The Corleones had the mob. We had basketball.

When I met him he was 24, an engineer who dressed well,

drove a Porsche, and had only one thumb. (He lost the other in a childhood accident, not as he claimed, playing hoops.)

All of that would change, except the thumb.

He told me what he really wanted was to teach high school and coach. Said he didn't care about making money, he wanted to make a difference, invest in lives. Yes, it was the '60s.

So he went to Berkeley to get a teaching credential, we were married on spring break, and in the fall of '69 he started teaching math at Monterey High.

Early on, he coached not only basketball, but football and baseball, too. I didn't see a lot of him, just enough to have three children.

They cut their teeth on bleachers. Our oldest played on Dad's team. Our daughter was a cheerleader. And our youngest, once when he was four, unplugged the scoreboard during a game.

Every year Coach would rate his team, either "We're not bad" or "We stink." "Not bad" was a championship. "Stink" could go either way. Seemed most games were won or lost by a free throw in overtime. While the crowd went nuts, the coach kept calm, crouching by the bench, deep in thought.

"What were you thinking tonight?" I once asked.

"I was thinking how to hide the hole I ripped in my pants," he said.

So many memories. The time his team shaved his head like a Hare Krishna's. The benefit basketball game with the 49ers when he stole the ball from Jerry Rice. A team dinner at our house when I dumped the roast in my lap. Stories I could tell, but won't here.

What I will say about the coach is this: He worked hard and cared deeply. Always.

Even the last two seasons while battling cancer.

He made a difference, invested in lives; so said countless former players and students who came to see him in the hospital, sent cards, or phoned. His career began and ended with championships: his first and last games were wins.

Not bad for a guy with one thumb.

A FINAL MEMORY: When his all-time best team lost a heartbreaker in the Northern California semifinals, he said, "The kids played their hearts out. Made me proud."

I say the same for the coach.

To My Kids, Who Aren't Kids Anymore
- May 12, 1997 -

Every mother's day I tell my children that they've given me more than I ever expected and I don't want them to waste money on an expensive gift.

It's one of the few things I've ever told them that they actually seemed to hear.

In truth, they are kind, thoughtful, generous souls, who would insist, no doubt, on spoiling me rotten, if only they weren't so broke.

The youngest, when he was six, gave me an IOU for Mother's Day: "Dear Mom, this is good for two billion bucks and kisses. You can have the bucks when I get rich. You can have the kisses any time."

For this Mother's Day, I've decided to write a column about some of the things they've given me, and to thank them for making me a mom.

To my three children, who aren't children anymore:

Your first gift to me was intimacy. I carried you inside my body, birthed you into the world, nursed you at my breast until you thrived. That may sound pretty gross to you now, but trust me, you loved it, almost as much as I did.

You let me change your diapers, walk the floor with you when you couldn't sleep, hover by your side to keep you breathing. Jesus said that to be great, we need to be servants. You made me feel like the greatest servant ever—Mother Teresa in faded jeans.

It was my hand you clung to when you took your first step, when you got your first stitches and fought back tears (yours and mine).

You let me sell hot dogs at your Little League games, sit through field hockey matches in the rain, and learn more about basketball than the head coach himself, as I often explained to him at dinner.

You locked in my memory my favorite smells—baby powder, gym socks, Play Doh, wet dogs, and the napes of your necks. Speaking of dogs, thanks for Maggie and Tuff. And for Fluffy the hamster, Rocky the cat, and Clancy the iguana, each an education in itself. Thanks for curing me of my squeamishness for lizards, tide-pool creatures, heavy metal, and the sight of blood. All those trips to the ER and the principal's office made me a wiser, if older, woman and taught me to be strong under fire and not to fall apart until the flames were out.

Thanks for never seeming to notice that the Halloween costumes I made were tacky, that the cookies I baked for school were burned, or that you never won a prize for selling candy because I wouldn't go door-to-door.

Thanks for always giving me an excuse to read to you or watch you play or take you to the beach, when I could have been doing the laundry.

Thanks for making me an expert on childhood diseases, California history, science projects, and stain removal.

Thanks for always being what I needed. For making me proud and keeping me humble. For showing me there are some things I can fix and a lot of things I can't. And for asking questions like, "If parents could turn out perfect kids, Mom, where did God go wrong with Adam and Eve?"

Thanks for becoming who you are, both because of and in spite of me. It's the only gift I need this Mother's Day.

But is it too much to expect a card?

Deliverance
- June 11, 1997 -

Lately we've had to rethink the options, such as they are, for my husband's treatment. Cancer is a maze. We are its rats. For three years, we've been running, picking a path, following it with conviction, until...

Wham!!!

We slam headlong into a wall.

Then we sit, dazed and confused, until once again, we catch a faint whiff of cheese. For the record, he is the rat who gets stuck with the needles. I'm the one who trots at his heels, nagging him to ask for directions, hoping for a pit stop soon.

If you've read this column often, you may be thinking, *Oh no, she's writing about cancer again.* I often think that myself. I've even given myself what my mother called a "good talking to" about it.

"Cancer is boring," I say, "nobody wants to read it and you don't want to write it. So write about something else, like movie stars or UFOs or, hey, write about dogs. People love to read about dogs. Go ahead. Do it. I dare you."

And I do. I write, not just about dogs, but other people, other lives for a while. Then I find myself, as I did just now, staring at the screen on my laptop, thinking, *Oh no, here I go again.*

So...

Today, instead of writing about cancer, I will write about John Muir. My husband, who grew up on a dairy ranch and camped every summer in the Sierra, fancies himself an outdoorsman. He likes nothing better than getting sweaty hiking in Yosemite. When he can't do that, he likes to read about Muir, who depending on your view, was either the greatest, sweatiest outdoorsman ever (and the father of our national park system) or a bedbug who ought to have been locked up.

A friend gave us the Muir biography by James Mitchell Clarke. My husband is so taken with it he insists on reading me passages aloud. Last night he read how Muir, climbing Mt. Ritter in 1872, got stuck between a rock and a hard spot—halfway up a 50-foot cliff "where there seemed to be no way to go farther."

There he clung, writes Clarke, to the face of the cliff, "unable to move hand or foot, either up or down. His doom appeared to him certain. He must fall. There would be a moment of bewilderment and then a lifeless rumble down the one general precipice to the glacier below."

Muir became "nerveshaken" and his mind "seemed to fill with a stifling smoke." Then, suddenly, the smoke cleared.

"Life seemed to blaze forth with preternatural clearness" and he became "possessed of a new sense." His muscles stopped trembling. He saw rifts in the cliff "as through a microscope" and moved with "a positiveness and precision" that seemed entirely independent of him. The deliverance, Clarke says, was as complete as "if he had been borne on wings."

I don't know what moved Muir on that mountain. Maybe he caught a whiff of cheese. But I know, as you do, what it's like to feel stranded, to be paralyzed by fear.

Sometimes, like Muir, all we can do is believe in the possibility of deliverance, and then believing, reach for it with all our might...

Next time, maybe I'll write about dogs.

Legends of the Falls
- June 30, 1997 -

Heading out the door for an appointment with my husband's doctor, I glanced at the clock to check the time and got splashed, so to speak, by Yosemite Falls. I laughed all the way to the office.

A clock that hung for years on our family room wall had to be moved recently to make way for a gift from our oldest.

Josh is out of college now, living in Los Angeles, so we don't see him often. When he comes home, he gets treated better than God. (God does His own laundry and doesn't eat half as much as the boy.)

On his last visit, just after Father's Day, Josh came in grinning, proud of himself and the gift he'd brought for his dad: a framed poster of a photograph of Yosemite Falls by Ansel Adams.

Have you ever given or been given the perfect gift? One that says, without saying, all that needs to be said, so clearly it needs no explanation?

This was that sort of gift. I could see it in their faces, in the look that passed between them, that lit up their eyes to the same shade of blue, the one that always makes my knees a little weak.

They have history, those two, with Yosemite Falls. One summer years ago, when we were camping in Yosemite Valley—as we have most every summer since we've been a family—my husband announced that Josh was a man, or darn near one, ready to join his dad in an assault on Yosemite Falls.

Josh was 12. Barely big enough to tie his own hiking boots and too young to know what he was getting into.

"Don't worry," said my husband, putting a snakebite kit in the boy's backpack, "he'll be fine. He's ready."

"I know he is," I said. "But what about you?"

They left at daybreak. Josh's pack looked bigger than his body. I snapped their picture and choked back tears.

Yosemite Falls is the highest waterfall in North America, some 2,400 feet from its rim to the valley floor. I had seen it frozen in winter, raging in spring, bone dry in summer and fall. But I'd never seen it as I did that day, all day, morning to twilight. I watched as nightfall swallowed it up. Then I closed my eyes and watched it in my memory.

Long after dark, they staggered into camp, starving, grinning, too tired to talk. I heard all about it in the days and years to come, story upon story, each grander than the last. They were a braver pair than Lewis and Clark, mightier than Batman and Robin, funnier than Bill and Ted.

The hike became a milestone in our family folklore, and a

metaphor for the relationship between the father and son: one leading by example, showing the way, the other following, trying hard to learn the pace.

We aren't going to Yosemite this summer. My husband is fighting cancer. He has bigger mountains to climb.

So for Father's Day, the boy brought Yosemite Falls—and a flood of memories—home to his dad.

I'm still not used to the change in the family room. I keep looking at the poster, expecting to see a clock, bracing myself for another reminder that time is racing by. Instead, I get picked up like Dorothy in *The Wonderful Wizard of Oz*, set down for one moment not in Kansas, but Yosemite, in sparkly red hiking boots.

Hope I never get used to it.

Swinging and Thinking
- July 14, 1997 -

Summers in my childhood were spent swinging. Sometimes I would perch like a bird in a tree, let the wind rock me to and fro. More than once, I almost hanged myself dangling from the end of a rope.

But most of the time, early morning, late at night, I'd curl up like a cat in a wide, wooden swing in the shelter that was my grandmother's front porch. I spent hours there swinging and thinking, trying to make sense of the world I'd been given, finding rhythm and order in chaos.

Can an eight-year-old do such as that? She can, given enough time to swing. It was a vastly different experience—the way floating in a pond differs from white-water rafting—from the action-packed, virtual reality sort of summer that children and their parents know today.

Boredom in itself is not always a bad thing, depending on how it is used. Children need time to have "nothing to do." Provided you don't leave matches in their reach.

I liked swinging alone. But I liked it even better with my grandmother. She had reared 12 children—grew their food, made their clothing, carried their water, chopped their wood. She could appreciate the value of having nothing to do.

We swung well together, she and I, like synchronized swimmers with perfect timing, no need to count the beat. I remember her arm cool against my cheek, and how she always smelled of lavender and snuff. Lavender was the scent of her talcum powder; snuff was the tobacco she packed in her lip.

I remember the creak of the chains that held the swing, the tap of our toes on the porch, the spit and zing of tobacco juice hitting the bottom of the can. But mostly I remember how my thoughts grew clearer, how my mind grew easier with swinging.

These days, I live on the coast of Northern California, where summers tend to be foggy and cold, and lighthouses are more common than porches. We bought a metal glider once, set it out on the deck. It rusted to dust overnight.

But last month, when my husband, a high school teacher, began his summer break, I went out and bought him a hammock. I assembled it myself, no tools required. It only took three days.

Fighting cancer tends to leave him with lots to think about and little energy for doing much else. So I gave him something for swinging and thinking, for trying to make sense of the world he's been given, for finding rhythm and order in chaos. Swell. All he does in the hammock is sleep.

Not me. I can swing in that thing forever, never bat an eye. Take the other night. He was torturing himself watching a game on TV where the Giants were hosting batting practice for "the stinkin' Dodgers." So I wrapped up in a blanket and went out to the hammock.

It was a spectacular evening. Great chunks of fog slid across the sky gobbling stars and spitting them out like seeds. I lay there an hour, dangling my foot to keep pushing, swinging, thinking.

Pretty soon, one by one, my thoughts grew clearer, my mind began to ease. And there for a moment, I could swear the air smelled of lavender and snuff.

Hand in Hand

- August 10, 1997 -

Went for a walk last night, my husband and I, bundled up like middle-aged Eskimos and holding hands like the skinny kids we were that summer of 1968, when we locked eyes and never looked back.

These days we hold hands more for safety than romance. We're not old, no, but we're not exactly agile. My husband is a cancer patient. And I am terminally clumsy. Picture Ricky Ricardo, seriously ill, with Lucy for a nurse.

Nevertheless, there is a kind of romance in safety—perhaps the truest kind of all—in feeling completely sure of someone; in knowing that, if you fall, he will be there to catch you. Or pick you up. Or go call 911. I've taken shelter in that feeling, that surety, for almost 30 years.

My husband was a lifelong jock, a high-school coach who ran a marathon the year before he turned 50 and discovered he had cancer. After three rugged years of treatment, he's happy just to be able to walk. And we have lots of time to walk now that he's decided not to teach this semester. He has always been big on excellence and diligence.

"You do a job well or not at all, give 100 percent," he says.

You know how jocks like to talk. But he walked his talk, gave his best every day, going from school to chemotherapy to basketball practice, then home to grade papers before bed.

Some days, he still thinks he could teach; other days, he barely has enough energy to channel surf with the remote. So he's staying home to pursue his new goal in life: trying not to drive his wife crazy.

It's a good goal, don't you think? I helped him set it. He's giving it 100 percent.

He reads. Does crossword puzzles. Watches baseball on TV. And he spends hours talking to people—friends and family, former students and players—who phone or come by to visit or take him on an outing.

I like those people a lot. So does my husband. He writes their names in his "thankful book," a daily list of people and things, shining graces for which he is grateful.

My name goes in there, too. Even when he drives me crazy and I threaten to hide the remote. He lists me second, right after God. Says God never hides the remote.

I am thunderstruck by this irony: The same disease that threatens to destroy us has given us more time together than we ever had before.

Last night on our walk the fog was thick as cotton, draped on trees like Spanish moss, softening streetlights to a misty glow and swirling around our feet. It reminded me of my senior prom, "Enchantment on the Bayou."

I know this neighborhood, every street, every dog. But in the dark, in the fog, it seemed entirely foreign. We walked for blocks, this way and that, past houses and apartments, homes of strangers and friends, until we came to an old two-story place with a beckoning oak and a rusty gate all but lost in the fog.

Lucky for us, we had left a light on.

Life seems dark sometimes, dense as a mist, swallowing up landmarks until we feel lost.

But with a good hand to hold onto, and a clear light in the window, sooner or later, we find our way home.

Key of Life

- August 31, 1997 -

The piano in our living room belonged to my husband's mother. She left it to him 30 years ago, when she died of cancer at the age of 43.

She left other things to her daughter, but the piano went to her son who had inherited, she said, her love for music—or at least sat through years of piano lessons while his sister refused to practice a lick.

Funny, isn't it? Children take or leave strengths and weaknesses from their parents, or even from generations long past—a dash of him, a sprinkling of her—mixing it all up in a genetic blender to create something new, all their own.

Our children took traits from both my husband and me, though not necessarily the ones we'd have chosen to give them, were it up to us.

The subject of who got what from whom is a frequent source of debate, especially now that the children are grown and itching to lay some blame. But on this much we agree: What they know about the piano, they owe entirely to their dad.

I grew up in a family that loved music, but had neither money nor patience for music lessons. We sang, but did not play instruments, assuming you don't count kazoos.

So it was my husband, not I, who held our babies in his lap and played his mother's piano while they banged on the keys with their fists.

It was he who insisted they take lessons, who nagged them to practice, who helped them when they asked for help, and who showed them by example how much fun it was to make music.

When they were little, he'd come home from teaching high

school and coaching basketball to sit for an hour and play piano, while they and their dog danced around the room bobbing and weaving like a flock of penguins.

Our youngest, who was then three, loved the game even after his brother and sister outgrew it. His favorite accompaniment was a rock 'n roll oldie that my husband called—and I am not making this up—"Mashed Potatoes One More Time."

"Play 'Mashalaters,' Daddy, one more time," he would beg. So my husband would play it again and again, sending the three-year-old into a funny little stomping frenzy with sparks of light shooting like fireworks from his blond curls.

I wish you could have seen them, both the pianist and the dancer. I'm not sure which one of them loved that game more.

Well, the baby grew up, as babies will, and though he was the most musical of our children, he refused to take music lessons, other than what he learned from his dad. And soon, their game was history.

My husband still played the piano for himself (or for me and the dog when he could corner us), turning page after page in song books and hymnals that once belonged to his mom.

Lately, however, it's been his turn to battle cancer—a fight that leaves him little energy for making music—and I've missed hearing him play.

But last night, while doing dishes, I heard the piano. Someone was playing "Mashed Potatoes One More Time." And it never sounded so good.

So I dried my hands and went out to the living room, where I found at the piano not my husband, but our son.

The Paper Cranes
- September 3, 1997 -

One of the more memorable books I ever read to my children was Eleanor Coerr's classic *Sadako and the Thousand Paper Cranes*.

Perhaps you know it. It is based on the true story of a Japanese child who was two years old in 1945 when the atomic bomb was dropped on Hiroshima, killing some 200,000 people. Some died instantly from the blast, others years later from radiation exposure.

The book tells how Sadako survived the bombing only to fall victim 10 years later to "atomic bomb sickness," a leukemia caused by radiation poisoning. She was visited at the hospital by a young friend who brought her an origami crane (crafted in the Japanese art of paper folding) and reminded her of a Japanese legend: Anyone who folds 1,000 paper cranes will be granted a wish for good health.

So Sadako began folding crane after crane, a tedious task that gave her purpose and hope, even as she grew weaker. When she died October 25, 1955, she had 644 cranes. Her classmates folded the other 356, so she could be buried with 1,000 paper cranes.

Three years later, a statue of Sadako—holding a golden crane—was placed in Hiroshima's Peace Park. Its inscription read: "This is our cry, this is our prayer: Peace in this world."

It's not an easy story to understand, for a child or an adult. When I read it to my children years ago, I tried to explain to them that prayer is answered in many ways, not always as we expect, and that peace can be found even in battle and healing can take place in life and in death.

I can't say they understood it then, although they nodded as if they did. But I think they understand it now as adults. They're always glad to explain it to me, any time I forget.

Last weekend, Amber, one of my husband's former students, called to ask if she and some classmates from Monterey High could bring my husband a gift.

He'd been their chemistry and physics teacher, their basketball coach and their friend. They had watched him battle cancer, had even talked with him about it in class. So this year, when he'd been too ill to resume teaching, well, said Amber, he was missed.

"Come on over," I told her, "he loves gifts."

And so they came, bringing 1,000 paper cranes in more colors than I'd ever imagined, each painstakingly folded, strung on fishing line and ready to hang in our den.

They also brought a video showing scores of teenagers folding tiny bits of paper and chanting, "Come back, Mr. Randall, we miss you!"

Always a man of few words, this time he was speechless. Finally, he summoned his best teaching voice and quoted a line from the card they had written for him: "We weren't sure if we could actually fold so many cranes. The fact that we did just proves the power of love, prayer, and caring."

"Remember that," he said, and they nodded as if they would. Then they sat at his feet, talking and laughing, with 1,000 paper cranes flying rainbows above their heads.

An End...and A Beginning

—

February 15, 1998 to May 24, 2001

I'd Hoped Not to Write This
- February 15, 1998 -

These are words I'd hoped never to write. And I have no idea how to write them.

I'll start with the cat. She showed up at Christmas, a yellow-eyed calico with a baby face and a "take nothin' off nobody" disposition.

"Go away," I said, "you can't stay here. We're dog people. We don't do cats."

She, of course, ignored me, pressed her nose to the window as if to say, "Hey, I'm here. Get used to it."

"Don't you dare let that cat in," I told my son. He's 20 and very smart about some things, but dumb as a stump about cats. "And whatever you do, don't feed her!"

He ignored me, too, fed her scraps and smuggled her up to his room after I went to bed. He thought I didn't know, but I did. I peeked in and found him sound asleep with the cat curled up and purring in the curve of his neck. She glared at me, female to female. "All right," I said. "You win."

It was not a good time to take in a pet. In some ways, it was the worst time of our lives. But I decided if that cat could comfort my boy, I would sell my blood to buy cat food. Whatever the price, comfort feels like a bargain.

For four years my husband had been fighting cancer. And now he was growing weaker with every day, wearier with every hour. We had reached, I knew, the final round of the fight. I hoped we might have a few months after Christmas. Turns out, we had three weeks.

People talk about being prepared for death, as if anticipating a loss might lessen it. But you can't know what you've lost until it's gone. Prepared or not, death is always a shock. I knew my husband was dying; and I still thought he would live forever.

Several people suggested, and I agreed, that I needed to tell you about his death, as I had so often written to tell you about his life.

There ought to be better words, a finer typeface for such occasions. But words are still words, death is still death and, well, there it is.

I also want to tell you, because so many of you have asked, that my children and I are fine, thank you. We are grieving as best we can, I think, each of us in our own ways, alone and as a family.

In the last four years, I often had the sense that I was walking on water—buoyed not just by my own faith, but by the prayers and concerns of so many good people. I have that sense still, even now, and I thank you for your part in it.

I'm taking a few weeks off because I have things to do: Write 5,000 thank-you notes; return 500 casserole dishes; survive my 50th birthday; and figure out who I am now that I am no longer who I was.

I have to learn a new vocabulary, to say "single" now, instead of "married"; "I" instead of "we"; "cat" instead of "dog." They're not bad words, just unfamiliar to me. I need time to get used to them.

I also need to decide on a name for this cat ... and the kittens that are due any day.

Backsliding
- April 5, 1998 -

Two months after my husband lost a four-year fight with cancer, I decided it was time to go back to church.

I'd not darkened the church doors, as my mother would say, since before Christmas, when my husband's failing health made it hard for him to leave the house, and hard for me to leave him alone.

After his death in January, I came down with what my doctor called a bad case of flu. Some people said it was exhaustion; others said, no, it was just a broken heart.

In any case, I took two rounds of antibiotics, downed buckets of chicken soup from neighbors and friends, and fed my soul with hundreds of good wishes that flooded my mailbox day after day.

Also, I slept more than I thought possible; a deep, dreamless sleep that left me weary and longing to sleep even more.

But then one Sunday, I woke to sunshine—a brief, shining respite in the dreariest winter of my life—and decided I had slept long enough. So I showered, dressed, and drove to church before I had time to change my mind.

Halfway between the car and the church vestibule it hit me: This would be my first time in almost 30 years to go to church without my husband. There'd been rare occasions when he was away at a coaching clinic or team camp. But those times I barely remembered. This one, I'd never forget.

So it goes for those of us who lose someone we love. Life becomes a series of firsts—the first Christmas, first birthday, first tax audit or whatever—the first times to be without someone we counted on being with forever.

I was thinking about that as I hurried, head down, high heels clicking across the street. My plan was to slip in the back unnoticed and leave before the final amen. God forbid I should draw a crowd and have people fuss over me.

I never got to the door. There on the sidewalk, before saints and sinners alike, I tripped—went down on one knee and skidded for what felt like several city blocks, shredding my nylons, my kneecap, and my dignity.

Traffic screeched to a halt. Tourists came running. Someone offered to call 911.

"No!" I said, hobbling back to my car. "It's fake blood. I'm a stuntwoman. I get paid to do this stuff."

Driving home, I remembered countless times I had tripped in high heels and been caught by my husband. This was my first big fall without him to catch me. It wasn't pretty, I told myself, but I survived it. And it gave me an excuse to skip church.

Weeks have passed and my knee is healing. It still aches sometimes with a pain unlike any I've ever known. A scar has formed where the flesh was torn away, a deep purple reminder of what was once part of me. It may fade in time, but I expect to wear it to my grave. I'm human. Healing is one of the things humans do best. And most of us have the scars to prove it.

Recently, I took my first walk without my husband—a good, long walk, hardly limped at all. Someday I might go for my first run without him.

And I will definitely go to church again. Maybe next week. But I will never wear high heels again. Probably.

Jellyfish, Sharks, and a Table for One
- April 8, 1998 -

When I told my sister I was going to Hawaii alone, you'd have thought I said I was going to hell in a handbasket.

"You are not!" she said.

"Am, too," I told her.

"Isn't it too soon?"

"It's never too soon to go to Hawaii," I said. "It's open all year-round."

"Don't get smart with me," she snapped. "You know exactly what I mean."

Yes. She meant that I had just lost my husband; that I'd been a widow less than two months; that I still cried so often, so copiously and unpredictably, that I'd given up on mascara; that I needed family and friends in ways I'd never needed them before.

"It's my anniversary," I said. "I was married 29 years ago this month. I figure I can celebrate here in the rain, or there in the sun. Which would you pick?"

"Aren't you scared?"

"Yes," I said. "I'm scared to death of jellyfish. And sharks. I hate sharks."

"Be serious," she said. "Won't you be lonely?"

"Probably," I said. "But I can be lonely even when I'm with people I love. Might as well do it in the sun."

Dead silence.

"Don't worry," I said. "If it gets too bad, I can always call you. Collect."

I had similar discussions with several friends, my mother-in-law, my three young-adult children and the clerk at the drugstore where I bought sunscreen.

Everybody knew something about loneliness. In the end, they all agreed I might as well go to Hawaii. And the clerk added, "Reapply your sunscreen every four hours, honey, and drink lots of those fruity drinks with the pretty little paper umbrellas."

Maui was sunny. The hotel was fine. The fruity drinks had pretty paper umbrellas. But the beach was posted—and I'm not making this up—with warnings about jellyfish.

As if I needed a warning.

I stayed out of the water until the morning of my anniversary, when I swam out past the breakers with my husband's snorkeling mask. We'd come here on our honeymoon, two skinny kids with our lives ahead of us, like the ocean, as far as we could see. I'd been afraid to put my face in the water.

"Relax," said my husband, "try to breathe slowly and see what you can see."

Good advice, then and now.

But this time, I didn't see a thing. The water was murky. Thick with jellyfish, I bet. I decided to call it a day.

So I crawled up on the beach and ordered myself a fruity drink with a paper umbrella. (I don't drink alcohol, and I think it's tacky to say "virgin" in reference to a beverage, so I just asked for a $5 Slurpee.)

That evening I had dinner at a table by the water. I watched the sun melt into the ocean, felt the night rise up cool on my neck. I dined alone, but ate enough for two.

I celebrated 29 years of a marriage that had been a study in grace. We'd been made better people by having been together; our world had been made a better place.

I rehearsed a few memories, good and bad, to tell our grand-children someday. And I felt grateful as never before.

Then I went back to the hotel room to call my sister.

Mama Was Right about One Thing
- April 15, 1998 -

Mama said there'd be days like this.

Actually, Mama said a lot of things, but she was right about this.

"You'll have children one day," she told me years ago as I tried to pry her hands off my ankles so I could catch a flight to California, "and they'll grow up and move off to some godforsaken place where you can't get hold of them when you need to."

"I'll call you," I said, free at last and running like a scalded dog for the gate.

"Mark my words," she shouted, "someday you will know how this feels!"

I did not mark her words. I didn't even remember them until I had children. Then my oldest grew up and moved off to godforsaken Los Angeles, and now I can't get hold of him when I need to.

We communicate by machines. I leave questions on his voice mail, or punch my number into his pager, and he calls me back when I'm out and leaves the answers on my recorder.

Even if we connect and talk for hours by phone, it's not what my mother meant. A phone can do surprising things if you push the right buttons, but it won't let you look into someone's eyes or smell his hair or feel his hug. It won't let you get "hold" of him. Least of all, when you need to the most.

Once, when my oldest was six, I lost him. We were Christmas shopping in the mall. He was The Big Brother, too big to hold my hand. His sister, age four, The Helper, was popping wheelies with the stroller from which my toddler, The Fugitive, was trying his best to escape. I knelt to tie down the toddler and when

I got up, his brother was gone.

It took two hours, four security guards, a team of Santa's elves, and countless years off my life to find him at the water fountain where he'd gone to get a drink.

"I knew you'd find me," he said. That was 20 years ago; to this day, when we go out, I make him hold my hand.

I can't describe that feeling, the awful realization that I could lose someone I couldn't imagine living without. I'll never understand how people survive such a loss; I only know that we do.

I had a taste of that feeling this morning when I took my oldest to the airport. He'd flown up from L.A. for Easter weekend. I'd bribed him home with a promise to put extra chocolate in his Easter basket. Also, I paid for his airfare. Otherwise, the boy was going to drive 10 hours round trip and be here barely long enough to do his laundry.

This way we had time to celebrate the holiday, watch three movies, eat four real meals, not to mention snacks, and finish five major loads of laundry. I drove him to the airport at 6 a.m. It was dark, cold, and raining hard.

No, I did not hang on his ankles. I simply looked in his eyes for a moment, maybe two, then pressed my face into his chest and felt the crush of his hug. When he hugs you, you know you've been hugged.

Then I watched him board a tiny plane that bumped along the runway, wings trembling, until it disappeared in a stormy sky.

His parting words were, "I'll call you."

He'd better, I told him. He'll have children someday.

Salvation in Strange Waters
- June 7, 1998 -

My brother says he holds no grudge from when we were kids jumping a barbed-wire fence and I tripped him and put a six-inch gash in his leg.

It's enough, he says, to know that I will one day burn in hell for it. I think he's joking. But I'm not sure.

He's the youngest of my mother's four children. I was seven when he was born. At 43, he is still my baby brother, even if we haven't been together much the 30 years since I left the South for California.

He was just a boy when he had to fly to my wedding, God bless him, with our mother, who sank her claws in his arm and screamed, "Lordy, Gaaawd, we're going down!" before the plane even left the ground.

He says he forgave me for that, too. But, again, I'm not sure. The scar on his arm is worse than the one on his leg.

After I married, I didn't go back to visit often. Seems I was always busy having babies or doing laundry.

In my absence, much to my surprise, without any help or guidance from me, my brother grew up to be a man. He finished high school, went to work as a carpenter and married his long-time sweetheart. (Her name is the same as mine, which can get a bit confusing, but I refuse to be called "Big Sharon.")

Pretty soon he was running his own business, wheeling and dealing, building palaces for rich people the way we once built playhouses in the woods.

My mother was so proud of him she could hardly stand it. But that didn't stop her from being who she was—a woman who could lash out as readily as she could love. They had a "falling out" that led to a "parting of the ways."

Never mind what it was over. The "what" seldom matters—or is even remembered—so much as the "how" and the "why." For my brother, it was enough. And for too long a time, they barely spoke to each other.

Two years ago, as she lay dying, I got him to come to her hospital room. Then I stood by his side, my hand on his big shoulder as he hugged her and told her goodbye.

Last winter when my husband died, my brother flew out for the service, along with his wife and our sister. They stayed with me a week, an immeasurable comfort. Before they left, we all agreed to take a vacation together.

So here we are in Mexico, the four of us. Big Sister and Little Sharon are napping in the sun. Baby Brother and I are playing in the water. I'm wedged into an inner tube, cool and mostly dry, while he steers me about the pool like a tugboat pulling a steamer.

We talk about our lives; houses he wants to build, stories I want to write. He tells me what it was like for him growing up poor, knowing people who thought he'd never amount to much.

It feels good, he says, grinning to know he proved those people wrong.

And I grin, too, because I know exactly how he feels.

Then we notice the sun is setting. Little Sharon and Big Sister have gone in to eat.

"Push me to the edge of the pool," I say, "so I don't have to get wet."

"Nah," he says, "I think I'm just gonna flip you."

So he does.

I get very wet.

I swallow half the pool.

But at least now I know I won't burn in hell alone.

Passing the Lantern
- September 6, 1998 -

M y boys, I swear.

When they were little, learning to walk, I would trot along behind them holding my hands like safety nets to catch them.

Now they do that for me.

Seriously. You don't want to hurt me. My boys could make toast of you and a truckload of Mike Tyson's bodyguards.

Sometimes I like it; other times I don't. I'm not sure if I want to thank them or tell them to bug off. It's probably how they felt 20-some years ago, when I was young and they were small and all seemed right with the world.

In those days I hovered too close—hooked a finger in the straps of their overalls or cupped their chubby elbows with my hands. They'd wrinkle their brows into little pink washboards, shrug off my grip and say, "No, Mommy, I can do it all by myself."

But if they fell—and they fell a lot—they expected me to catch them. If I missed and they went flying headlong across the floor, after they stopped crying they'd give me a look, all teary-eyed and pitiful, more surprised than disappointed, as if to say, "So, where were you?"

It was hard for me to find a balance, to know when to hover and when to let go. Now it seems it's hard for them to find a balance between wanting to protect me and knowing I have to learn to walk again—this time, all by myself.

I began to notice it a few weeks ago. We went camping together, the three of us, our first time to do so since their dad died last winter. Without a word, the boys took on chores that had been mainly his—hauling in the gear, setting up the camp, finding just the right spot to hang the lantern.

Watching them, I was in awe. All those years, they seemed so clueless. Now they looked as if they'd been camping all their lives. Which, in fact, they had.

I guess some people don't show their tickets until they have to get on the train.

That whole week, wherever I went, my two boys went with me—to the camp store for groceries, to the beach by the river, even to the bathroom late at night, waiting for me outside with a flashlight.

When bears plundered the camp, the boys said, "Mom, get behind us." And I did.

When the wind scattered my newspaper, they said, "We'll get it." And I let them.

And when a 40-pound insect flew into my sleeping bag (and I had, yes, a hissy fit), instead of laughing at me as they would have not so long ago, they went after the poor thing like ducks on a June bug. And I cheered.

As I said, sometimes I like having my boys look after me. Other times, I think, hey, I can do this all by myself.

Finding a balance. Isn't that always the trick?

The last day we camped, I ditched the boys and sneaked off to the river to sit alone for a while. It was good.

But pretty soon they came looking for me, plodding along the beach, scanning the river, shading their eyes from the sun. Something about the way they walked—so sure-footed, so funny, so much like their dad—made me want to laugh.

My boys, I thought, shaking my head. Then aloud, I said, "No. My men."

Bioluminescence
- June 23, 1999 -

This is an evening that I've been longing for. I always look forward to going home, as we say, to visit my family in the South. It's good medicine to be with blood kin and lifelong friends—to look in their eyes and remember who I am, to laugh and eat and sing and dance and reminisce about old times.

That's the main reason I get back home as often as I can; I like these people. You would, too, if you knew them. But they're not the only draw that pulls me back to a place that, 30 years ago, I couldn't wait to flee.

Go figure. Why do some of us spend the first 20 years of our lives trying to break free of our roots (whatever those roots might be) only to spend the rest of our lives trying to get them back? Home for me has always been found in the eyes of people I love. I find it coast to coast, wherever those people happen to be scattered, from the mountains of North Carolina where I was born, to the coast of Northern California, where I've spent 30 years, reared three children, and lived the life of my dreams.

But given my druthers, come summer, I'd rather feel at home in the South, mostly for the evenings. Days are a different story; I prefer them in the fall, when they aren't hotter than the gates of hell. But I will forever be hopelessly partial to warm Southern nights.

When we were children, my cousins and I spent most summer evenings, weather permitting, running barefoot on wet grass, squishing snails between our toes and chasing lightning bugs just to see if we could catch them.

Which we could, even the littlest cousins. Lightning bugs, like some humans I've known, are lovely to look at, but they're slow. They light up, but they're not bright.

If you caught one, you could put it in a jar with a few air holes in the lid. (Lightning bugs need air not just to breathe, but to make light, a kind of magic called "bioluminescence," one of my all-time favorite words I wouldn't learn until years later.)

If you couldn't find a jar, you could cup them in your hands and wave your fists like lanterns.

Lightning bugs have lots of uses, especially in the mind of a child. My favorite way to use them was as carriers for my prayers.

I would catch one in my hands, just so, and when I was sure my cousins weren't watching, I'd whisper a prayer in the general direction of what I believed to be the bug's ear. This took a lot of faith, not because I was talking to an insect—I had no doubts about that—but because I could not see the ear. Or even be sure the bug had one.

But I didn't let that stop me. Like any child, I prayed for my parents and grandparents—for their happiness and safety—the same prayers I now pray for my children.

I took all the things I hoped for, and all the things I feared, and sent them flying off to God on the wings of a bioluminescent bug. And every flash of light I saw was counted as an answer to a prayer. Maybe I should've had analysis as a child. Wonder if it's too late?

I've lofted prayers on other flying things, too, at other times and places in my life: on birds and kites and butterflies, on falling leaves and shooting stars and swirling fog. And more than once, when my husband lay ill, on the wings of angels dressed as doctors and nurses.

But tonight, sitting on my sister's porch in Carolina, with a glass of iced tea in my hands and a warm Southern breeze on my

neck, I'm pinning my prayers to the wings of lightning bugs.
Look.
Did you see that flash?

My First Official Date in 30 Years
- July 24, 1999 -

The E-mail note from my 17-year-old niece was brief, she said, because she had to get ready for a really big date. Then in typical Jessie-fashion, she summed up her feelings and mine: "Pretty scary, huh?"

Jessie doesn't know how lucky she is to be an only child. She could have had my sister and brothers, who made dating such an inferno for me it's a miracle I'm not a nun.

My sister, who is five years older than I am, is a merciless tease. She claims when she was dating, I was such a little brat (not true, I was actually big for my age) that she vowed to pay me back some day. And pay me back she did, a thousand times over.

Imagine a grown, married woman persecuting her poor little sister with "Who is he? What's he like? Where's he taking you? When's he bringing you home?"

And the one question that never failed to make me go ballistic, "How many times are you going to let him kiss you?"

It was actually a tag-team effort. My sister handled the warm-up matches until my date showed up, then she would signal Monkey Boy into the ring. His specialty was to hide behind the couch and make, well, indelicate sounds with his armpit.

But the corker was that my brother Joe, who was born blind, would then insist on running his hands over my dates just to see what the poor guys looked like.

I got married 3,000 miles from home, far from the tag team's reach. I never planned on getting back in that ring. Never planned to lose my husband, either. But in the five years he fought cancer—and in the 18 months since he lost that fight—I've tried to plan less and live more.

My grandmother used to say that if you want to hear God laugh, tell him about your plans. I've heard God laugh a lot lately. It was only fitting, I guess, that I'd find my way full circle—back to my hometown and the ever-watchful eyes of my family—for my first official date in 30 years.

At least I had enough sense not to tell my brothers. But the big mistake was telling my sister. She laughed even louder than God.

"We'll get the whole family here to see you off," she chirped "and we'll make lots of pictures. It'll be just like the prom! I'd better go buy you a corsage, in case he forgets."

"Keep it up," I said.

She did. All day. Teasing and torturing just like old times. As if I needed to be, like, a little more nervous. I was sweating so hard I couldn't dry my hair or get my makeup to stick or dial the phone to cancel.

I was almost out the door when she pulled, once again, the old "who is he, what's he like, where's he taking you, when's he bringing you home, and how many times are you going to let him kiss you?" routine.

"OK," I said. "Fine. You want answers? Here goes: (A) a friend; (B) very nice; (C) out to dinner; (D) when I'm good and ready; and (E) none of your business."

"Be home by 11," she yelled after me laughing, "or you're grounded!"

The next time I E-mail my niece I will tell her a few things: First, being an only child has certain advantages.

Second, dating is a lot like life: it can be scary at any age— whether you're 17 and going on a really big date, or 51 and going on your first real date in 30 years.

But it can also be a lot of fun.

And finally, I will tell her that getting grounded is not so bad—especially if it's for a good cause.

Fisherman's Daughter
- August 10, 1999 -

The Davidson River in North Carolina winds like a ribbon out of the Blue Ridge Mountains, past the Pink Beds, over Sliding Rock, beyond the Cradle of Forestry, and directly into my heart.

Once, long ago, I believed it was the only river in the world— the only one that mattered—though I don't know why, exactly.

The things that matter to us as children don't always make sense when we grow up. But lately, for whatever reasons, I've been trying to make sense of all sorts of things that I had long left unattended. My friends say it's because I'm getting old. I say, they should know.

It has been years, almost a lifetime, since I last saw the Davidson. Somehow it looks different to me now, not as deep or wide as I remember it in my childhood, but I doubt that it has changed quite as much as I have. I wonder if it remembers me.

My daddy liked to fish in this river. He liked to fish anywhere, really, but he was partial to the Davidson, where he learned to cast a line before he learned to crawl, he said, and where he tried hard, but failed, to make a fisherman of me.

I loved my daddy dearly, but I truly hated to fish.

Fishing, he told me, took patience, something I was short on as a child and am not long on even now.

You had to sit still to fish, he'd say, and if you wanted to catch something worth keeping, you shouldn't even fidget.

I didn't care if I caught anything worth keeping or not, and try as I might to sit still, fidgeting was, as he put it, my middle name.

You shouldn't talk while fishing, either, he said, at least not much louder than a whisper, or else you would scare off all the fish.

Sometimes, when we'd go home empty-handed, he would use me as an excuse, telling anybody who would listen, "We didn't fish much today, but we sure talked a lot."

I knew he was saying I had scared off the fish. Children are not always quite as dumb as their parents seem to think. But knowing didn't stop me from talking. I had too many things I wanted to tell him and too little time for telling.

After he and my mother parted ways when I was two, I got to see him only on occasional weekends or for a week or so in the summer when I visited him and my grandparents on their farm near Pisgah Forest.

Some of the happier hours of my childhood were spent here with him. And I'd have been even happier if he hadn't tried to make me fish.

By the time I was 10 he knew it was useless—didn't even bother to bait my hook. But he still made me go fishing with him.

It might not have been so bad if he at least had been willing to talk. But he liked to talk the way I liked to fish, meaning, of course, not at all.

We made, he said, quite a pair.

Sometimes, when I grew weary of the sound of my own voice, I would settle down beside him and watch the river gliding by. Once in a while, if I watched long enough, I'd find myself strangely content to be, not a fisherman, but a fisherman's daughter, seeing our reflections dance on the water and listening to angels sighing in the trees.

I never told him that, of course. He would have tried to make me go fishing with him more often.

But maybe I'll tell him that today when I stop by the cemetery to pay my respects and pull a few weeds from around his headstone before going home to California.

If I had a pole right now and some decent bait, I could cast a line in memory of my dad (in that pool I see over by the riverbank, that's the kind of spot he'd always pick) and I'm pretty sure I would catch something worth keeping.

I could do that, but I won't. I'm a fisherman's daughter, and proud of it, too. But I still hate to fish.

Sleeping with Sissy
- October 29, 1999 -

S omewhere in a dream, I hear my sister saying, "Wake up, Sissy. Look outside."

I hide my face in the pillow.

I am 9 years old and she is 14. We share a room, a bed, a mother who means well, and a life that isn't easy, but could be worse.

In another year she will be gone, my big sister, my champion—gone from this house with its cracked walls and icy floors to find a life of her own—leaving me a bed to myself and a big empty hole in my heart.

But she is here now, beside me, in this bed, in this dream, telling me to look outside, and so I do.

It's snowing.

Has been all night, I would guess. The ground lies buried a foot deep or more. The tall weeds by the trash pile have all but disappeared. Snow clings to everything, every place I look—to the limbs of the trees in the apple orchard, the ties on the railroad tracks, the burrow where the rats hole up in the pasture, even to the barbs on the barbed wire fence.

The sky is gray, hanging its head so low you can almost reach up and touch it, sifting silver-dollar snowflakes the way my mother sifts powdered sugar on a cake.

And everything, everything is silent, silent.

Listen. Can you hear it? It's as if, for the moment, the world and all within it—the birds in their nests, the rats in their hole, me and my sister, and God and all His angels—are wrapped up safe and warm in a white downy quilt.

I study it carefully. I take it all in. I accept it for the gift that it is. Then I turn to my sister, sitting cross-legged and smug on the bed beside me, as if somehow this were all her doing, and together we shout two of the loveliest words any child has ever known: "No school!"

That's not just a dream. It's a memory. I visit it often, waking or sleeping, like medicine, as needed.

Apparently, I need it now.

"Wake up, Sissy," I hear my sister say in a fog. "Look outside."

So I hide my face, as usual.

But wait. Something is wrong.

That is my sister's voice. I'd know it anywhere. But it surely doesn't sound 14. The bed doesn't sag. The springs don't creak. And my legs and arms are too long.

Suddenly I'm awake. This is not a dream or a memory. It's real.

My sister is standing beside the bed. She's no teenager. And I am no child. This is her house. I am visiting again. We have our own lives on opposite coasts. Our mother is gone, our children are grown, and we can't be together as often as we'd like. But we're together now, if for only a few days, and she is telling me to look outside, so I do.

It's snowing.

Has been all night, I would guess. The ground lies buried, just a few inches deep, and the little white car I rented at the airport has all but disappeared.

Snow clings to everything, everywhere I look. To the blooms on the big cherry tree that was just a twig when she bought this place. To all those juniper bushes she made me help her plant. To the porch where we sat late at night, she and I, talking and laughing and watching lightning bugs, that summer after my husband died. To her "bubba" truck parked in the driveway.

Even to the giant backhoe she borrowed when she was in the mood to move some dirt.

The sky is gray, hanging its head, sifting snow like sugar.

And everything is silent.

Listen. Can you hear it?

It's as if, for the moment, the world and all within it is wrapped up, once again, safe and warm.

I study it carefully. I take it all in. I accept it for the gift that it is.

Then I turn to my sister, standing over me cross-armed and smug, as if this were all her doing, and together we shout two of the loveliest words any adult has ever known: "Let's eat!"

The snow will melt tomorrow. I'll go home to California. And I'll have another memory to dream on.

Toilet Repair
- November 2, 1999 -

Standing in my bathroom in a small puddle of water, with a pipe wrench in my hand and a big grin on my face, I was struck by the following thought:

This has been a memorable year. I've had so many firsts I can't begin to list them. What? OK, fine, I'll list a few. Let's see, there was, um...well, never mind, I forget right now, but trust me, there were lots of them. And the year isn't over yet.

But no matter what else happens—even if I win the lottery, which is not too likely as I never buy a ticket and even if I did

I wouldn't win—I will always remember 1999 as the year that I single-handedly fixed a leak in my toilet.

Maybe you fix your plumbing every day, but for me, this was a first, and I am proud of it. Actually, it wasn't a leak; the water in the tank just ran all the time, which, if you know anything about toilets, is not something you really want. Especially if you ever care to sleep or pay your water bill. When I first noticed the problem, I responded at once with my usual take-charge approach: I ignored it.

Sometimes, if you ignore things, they'll just go away. Or somebody else will take care of them. Not true with toilets. Not at my house. At least, not any more.

For most of my life, until my husband died last year, I never thought much about toilets, aside from how to keep them clean with two boys and a man in the house. If I noticed a leak, I simply reported it to my husband. Spoiled as that may sound, I was not irresponsible. I carried my share of the marital load. Toilets were just his thing.

He'd get that grimace on his face, grab a pipe wrench and a bunch of other tools, shut off the water supply to the house, then disappear in the bathroom for a few hours or several weeks, but always, he would fix it.

I asked him once why he needed a pipe wrench. He said, "If I can't fix the leak, I can smash the toilet."

Anyhow, this week, when I could no longer ignore the Chinese water torture in my bathroom, I asked myself the question I've been asking all my life, especially in the last few years: How am I going to do this?

It used to be a rhetorical question, an expression of doubt and fear and agitation more than simple curiosity. But somewhere along the road it began to change—slowly at first, in fits and starts, until there was no going back. These days when I say, "How am I going to do this?" I'm not questioning whether I'll be able to do it; I'm just wondering if I'm going to need the pipe wrench.

You might call it experience. I like to call it faith—faith in myself and in the people who have faith in me, and faith in the God who is faithful, whether I am or not.

I had no experience whatsoever with plumbing. But I've learned a thing or two about this business of life, which is a whole lot messier than trying to fix a leaky toilet.

When your mother hurts you as only a mother can; when your father takes his life; when you fear your children will never come home and then, that they'll never leave; or when your husband dies and you wake up one morning and realize the stupid toilet is running. You still say, "How am I going to do this?" only now it's a prayer more than a question. And you don't sit around waiting for an answer.

To the Moon
- November 19, 1999 -

For a long time—or maybe just for a few minutes that felt like forever—I watched as his plane disappeared on the horizon and tried to tell myself that I'd done the right thing by encouraging him to go.

The boy has no idea how lucky he is to have me. If he'd had my mother, God rest her soul, she'd still be hanging onto his ankles. He'd have never gotten on that plane without her trying to stop him—just the way she tried to stop me.

My mother never understood how her children could choose to leave her, or why on earth we would even want to go to some faraway place with a strange sounding name where people talked funny, didn't eat right, and weren't even Baptists.

I was 20 the first time I tried to board a plane and my mother threw a fit. When I told her I was going to California, you'd have thought I said I was going to the dark side of the moon.

Or maybe to Nepal. That's where Nate's headed. He wants to spend a month backpacking from village to village, boiling his water and sleeping on the ground. I'd love to hear what my mother would have to say about that. It's probably just as well she doesn't know.

He began planning the trip last winter while in Yosemite National Park, where he'd gone to work for a year and do some thinking, he said, after he lost his dad to cancer.

When he told me his plans about Nepal, I bit my lip and didn't say a word. OK, maybe I said a couple of words, but nothing close to what my mother would've said.

I didn't say, for example, that I'd miss him. Or that I'd worry about him. Or that ever since his dad died, he and his brother and sister have become even more precious, more indispensable than I ever imagined anything could be. Or that if, God forbid, anything should happen to one of them, my life would go on, but I'm not sure how I'd breathe.

I didn't say any of those things. Didn't feel them necessary. I had no idea he could actually save all the money he needed for the trip. And yet somehow, even when he was a baby, I had a feeling that he'd do this—that he'd take off one day on some grand adventure and leave me waving from an airport window.

When he was two, every time I had to leave him, which was

not very often and never for very long, he would say, "Hurry back, Mommy, 'cause I will cry for you."

I almost said that to him at the airport while we were waiting for his flight. I thought it seemed only fair. Instead, I bought cinnamon rolls and a couple of lattes so we could eat and not talk for a while. Sometimes when everything's been said, it's best just to shut up.

Every generation needs its own big adventure. My mother seldom went more than 10 miles from home. But she got a divorce when she was 25. And that was further, said her mother, than anyone else in the family had ever dared to go.

I needed to go California. And I guess my boy needs to go to Nepal.

He isn't a boy any more, of course. He's 22, older than I was when I married his dad. But he's still my youngest, my baby.

When I reminded him of that at the airport, he laughed and wrapped his big arms around me the way I used to wrap mine around him when he was small.

And he promised to call me when he gets to Kathmandu.

I don't think I've ever had a call from Kathmandu before. But I don't expect to hear from him soon. I figure it'll take about as long to fly to Nepal as it would to ride a rocket ship to the dark side of the moon.

Which is probably where his children will want to go someday.

This Close
- November 29, 1999 -

I'm lying in my daughter's bed in San Jose, where she goes to college, watching her sleep in a pool of moonlight and feeling as a mother more blessed than the Virgin Mary.

This is big. I haven't slept with my daughter since she was a little girl. And I'll not likely do it again soon, after she reads this column. So I intend to enjoy it. I lie very still, resisting an urge to pull her close and nuzzle her neck.

I'm no fool. If I move one inch closer to her side of the bed, she'll go off on me like a car alarm and one of us will end up sleeping on her couch.

When she was not quite a year old, she decided she did not want or need to go to bed—ever—and that apparently, neither did her mother. She made this abundantly clear.

Every night, I'd bathe her, put on her nightgown, read her favorite story ("Goodnight Moon," at least twice), say her prayers, and nurse her until she fell asleep.

Finally, when she lay limp in my arms, I would ease her into her crib and try to slip out of the room.

Never once did I get past the door. She would bolt upright, screaming "No leave me, Mommy!" and shake that crib until it danced.

The pediatrician told me I should let her cry for a while.

"How long?" I asked.

"Long as it takes," he said.

So I tried it and it worked. Until she started banging her head on the wall. The pediatrician said to let her bang away, it wouldn't hurt her.

I said, fine, I'd bring her over and let her bang away at his house.

Instead, I'd put her to bed and sit by her crib—where she could see me and sing to me and babble on in that strange tongue spoken only by babies and angels—until she fell asleep. Sometimes, I'd linger after she slept to watch her eyes move behind their silvery lids, to see her smile like the Mona Lisa and wonder what she was dreaming. It made me want to pick her up and hold her close and nuzzle her neck. But as I mentioned, I'm no fool. It was enough just to watch her sleep. And to get a little sleep myself.

Some months ago, she called me long distance on her cell phone at 2 A.M. and said she had just been in an accident. She was standing beside a freeway with cars whizzing by and as hard as it was to hear her, I could tell that she was crying. She'd tried to call 911, she said, but couldn't get an answer, so she'd called me.

"Where are you?" I said. The line went dead. I waited. And I prayed. Two long minutes later, she called back with her location. I told her to get as far off the road as she could. When the line went dead again, I hung up, grabbed my cell phone and called the CHP in San Jose.

The next time she phoned, I could hear sirens. I didn't start crying until she stopped. She'd be OK, she said, not to worry. I made her stay on the line until the CHP arrived. An hour later she called again to say her car was totaled, but she was fine.

That's an old story now, but I still like to tell it. Stories of grace and deliverance ought to be retold. Funny, how clearly I remember it, as if it happened only yesterday.

I drove up to San Jose today to spend the night, at my daughter's invitation, with her and all her roommates. "You never come to see me, Mom," she said, and so I came, you bet, as fast as I could. Now I'm lying here beside her, wondering what she's dreaming, longing to tell her how much I adore her, wanting to pull her close and nuzzle her neck.

But I'm still no fool.

It's enough to watch her sleep.

And to know that I am blessed.

The Heart Is a Muscle
- March 19, 2000 -

They say the heart is a muscle, like your arms or your legs, and you either use it or you lose it. That's what I was thinking about this morning as I lay in bed half asleep trying to resist a growing urge to strangle the cat.

Yes, that would be the cat that I didn't want. She usually sleeps in my son's room, which serves him right for ignoring me two years ago when I told him not to feed that stray or we'd never see the last of her. This morning for some reason she ended up on my face. When I protested, she gave me one of those catty looks that says, "I am a cat. I kill for pleasure. Mess with me and you die."

I refuse to be bullied by a dumb animal. But this is one smart cat. She doesn't quite talk, but she communicates very effectively. When her ears slick back against her head, for example, and her tail starts cracking like a bullwhip, that means it is time for me to say, "Yes, ma'am," and do as I'm told.

I don't think she liked me much at first. And I admit the

feeling was mutual. Maybe we were just being cautious. Clearly she was in love with my son and saw me as the other woman. And I tend to be wary of things that make me bleed.

But the cat had some major issues. I'm not sure what they were or how she might've been mistreated but it has been quite an education to watch her slowly learn to trust. My boy is a miracle worker. He healed that cat, gave her whatever it was she needed, and in some ways, she did the same for me.

When you spend 30 years of your life learning to love—working at it day and night, longer and harder and with more blood, sweat, and tears than any runner ever trained for a marathon—you get to be pretty good at it. And the thing about love is, the more you give it away, the more you have to give. It wells up inside you until you think you're going to burst. Sort of like breast-feeding, it's all about supply and demand. Then one day you wake up and realize that most of the people you loved in your life are either grown or gone. When did that happen? And there you sit in an empty family room with a house full of scrapbooks, five sets of dishes, and this enormous capacity for love. It's not a bad place to be, if you can figure out what to do with it.

Everywhere I go I meet people like me, who for whatever reasons find themselves at that ironic stage of life where, just when they have so much to give, they seem to have so few places left to give it. They tell me about how lonely they are, how dearly they miss the lives they had, how much they long for companionship.

I understand those feelings. Loss is loss, the circumstances vary, but the feelings are much the same. I listen and try not to say much usually, because most people need you just to hear them out far more than they need your advice. But sometimes I want to say this: No one can tell you when to love again. You alone have to decide that. But pay close attention because that time will come. When it does, you'll want to be ready.

All those years you spent loving were the best investment of your life. You don't want to waste it. It served a purpose once, and it will again. Take all the time you need to grieve, but not a minute more.

And when you are through with grieving, please, choose life. Be alive. Go out and find somebody or something to love—be it a cause, a person, a convertible, or a cat—and then love like crazy, like you really mean business, like you have never loved before.

The world needs all the love that we can give it, and then some. And the heart is a muscle that we either use or lose.

The Dragon
- March 29, 2000 -

She comes home from college, my daughter who doesn't need me for much of anything anymore, except my money or her hair. We are standing at the mirror in my bathroom where we have stood countless times over the years waging a never ending battle to do anything at all on God's green earth to get the dragon to behave. As usual, I'm losing the fight. "What is that?" she says.

"What is what?" I ask, dumbly.

"The piece you left sticking up that makes me look like a rooster."

"Oh, that," I say. And then, once again, for the 10th time in the past 20 minutes, I untwist the French twist that I have coiled on her head and start all over again.

"Try to do it like you did the last time," she says, "but without the rooster thing. And make it tighter, so it won't fall down." Believe me, I am trying. Interesting, isn't it, the things we do to stay close to those we love? With my oldest, the actor, I talk movies. With my youngest, who likes to cook, I eat. My daughter and I have lots in common but we are bound for life by her hair.

Unlike her brothers, who were born hairless as a couple of cue balls, she came into the world looking ready for a party with wide blue eyes and thick, black curls. Which promptly fell out (the curls, not the eyes).

Six months later she was still bald as a cue ball. Then one day, like magic, her hair began to grow. And it grew and grew until it became a thick, golden, fire-breathing dragon hellbent on ruling our lives.

I remember how excited I got the first time I pulled it up in a little pouf on her head and pinned it with a tiny pink barrette. She looked absolutely adorable. Until she ripped out the barrette and tried to swallow it. Looking back, I can see it was an omen.

When she was three, the dragon divided rather nicely into two innocent-looking "puppytails," which I tamed and retamed countless times a day.

When she was six, it took the form of long stiff braids that flew like pennants as she rode her bike. In middle school, we tried everything short of sacrificing a live chicken to get the dragon to lie sleek on her head. And it would. For five minutes. Then it would coil up and hiss at me like Medusa's snakes.

In high school, we tried to perm it. Big mistake. Huge. Almost as big as the mistake I made when by some miracle I managed to French braid it. She liked it so much she made me do it every day before going to school with her dad, no matter how late it made him for his first class. Sure, he was his little girl's knight in shining armor, but he was no match for the dragon. I remember all the proms when the dragon reared its ugly head. She'd come home hysterical after a $75 appointment with a hair stylist shrieking as if she were on fire, "Mom! Help me! Do something!"

And here's what I would do: I would speak very softly, approach it very slowly—like Marlin Perkins slipping up on a Cape water buffalo—and I'd take it all down, hairpin by hairpin, curl by curl, tangle by tangle, tear by tear. I'd brush it free from all the hairspray, the gel and mousse and frustration, and calm it as best I could. And then, by the grace of God, I would do the impossible—find a way, no matter how long it might take, to tame the dragon to my daughter's satisfaction. I did that when she was little. I do it now, though she is big. And I hope to be doing it in a rest home someday when she comes to visit. "How's that?" I ask, on the twentieth French twist attempt.

Slowly she turns her head side to side, glowering at the dragon.

"Not bad," she says, "I like it," and rewards me with a quick hug.

Sometimes, to a mother, even a dragon can be a blessing in disguise.

The Cowboy Is Getting Married
- April 9, 2000 -

When he was little, my oldest child, who is very big now, wanted to be a cowboy.

I don't know where he got the idea. There were no cowboys on either side of the family, and none that I knew of in the neighborhood where we lived. He didn't see them on TV or in the movies the way his dad and I did when we were kids. He loved "Rocky and Bullwinkle," but that didn't make him want to grow up to be a moose or a flying squirrel. He wanted to be a cowboy. Dreamed of riding the range.

Where do dreams come from? And where do they go?

The Christmas when he was three, his grandparents gave him a rocking horse that was almost as big as our Volkswagen bus. He named it Flash. It was mounted on giant springs that stretched like rubber bands any time he rode especially hard, meaning any time he and Flash were awake. I lived in fear that someday one of Flash's springs would snap and launch the boy into orbit. When I told him that, his eyes grew wide and his mouth dropped open and he whispered, "Neato burrito!" Then he rode harder than ever.

One day, when I picked him up from preschool, he looked me square in the eye and said he wanted me to make him a cowboy vest.

"I don't sew," I told him.

"I know," he said. "I'll help."

So we went to a fabric store and bought a furry fake cowhide, took it home and, with his help, made a cowboy vest. Sort of. He loved it. Wore it day and night, even to bed.

I was sitting on his bed one night, having read once again his favorite part of Rudyard Kipling's *Rikki Tikki Tavi*, where the brave little mongoose fights an evil cobra "with tooth and jump and spring and bite" to save his young master's life. We were about to say prayers when suddenly the boy frowned.

"Mom," he said, "when I'm big, can I be a cowboy here? I never see any cowboys around here. And I don't ever wanna leave you."

A moment later, when I was able to speak, I told him there were cowboys in Carmel Valley and he could commute to work. That was 25 years ago. I remember it well, just as I do all the memories he made for me. The lizards he caught. The cooties he feared. The papers he delivered. The free throws he always made. I remember how scared he got the first time I took him to see Santa. How sick he was when he was 12 and had to have his tonsils out. How young he looked the first season he played basketball for his dad in high school. And how tall, how strong, how brave he was when I leaned on his arm and felt it hold me up, two years ago at his father's funeral. I remember it all as clearly as the recent evening when he called me on a cell phone from a restaurant in Hollywood to tell me he'd just proposed to the girl of his dreams.

He grew up to be an actor, not a cowboy (though he played one once in a movie). And he lives in Los Angeles, not at home with me.

Now he's getting married to a gorgeous young woman whom I already love like a daughter. And I will do my very best to make her love me, as well.

His horse is out to pasture in my garage. His vest is tucked away in my cedar chest. His copy of *Rikki Tikki Tavi* is lying on my shelf. But his heart is in LA with her.

And that, of course, is as it should be. She holds his future.

But I still have his past.

I figure, if I play my cards right—if I try just as hard to be a good a mother-in-law for her as I have tried to be a mom for him—with any luck, maybe we can share.

How the Music Plays On
- September 17, 2000 -

Standing here beside him, I realize how well I know his hands—every line, every crease, every scar on every knuckle—about as well as I know my own. But I didn't see the difference, never noticed it, really, until I heard him laugh and ask a room filled with guests, "Where's my mom?"

Now he's offering me his hand and leading me out on the dance floor and suddenly I spot it—something new, yet old, something strange, and yet familiar. For a moment, I can't see anything else.

We have danced together before, countless times over the years. But this dance, like this day, is a first for us both, different from any day and any dance we've ever known. And I've known him all his life.

When he was born, his hands seemed tiny, but huge, like a King Kong action figure scaled to size. His father, an ever-hopeful high school basketball coach, stared in awe at his firstborn's fat fingers and said, "Whoa. The little guy could get to be pretty big."

More than just big, the boy's hands were strong. He would clamp them on some part of me—flesh, hair, clothing, jewelry, anything in his reach. Then he'd cling to me like a cat that was getting flea-dipped, as if his life depended on it, as if he needed me as much as he needed air to breath and breast milk to guzzle and diapers to dirty by the dozens.

I had never had that effect on anyone before and for some reason, I rather liked it. But I especially liked watching him learn to use his hands. Sometimes he'd wave them in the air like a conductor directing a symphony and make me wish I could hear the music that was playing in his head.

When he was hungry, which was most of the time, he'd ball his hands up into fists and try his best to suck them dry, then get furious because he didn't like the taste.

He would practice catching light rays and moonbeams and dust particles and house flies, then sit quietly for an hour using his fingers like chopsticks to move Cheerios and frozen peas and little chunks of cheese from his high-chair tray into his mouth.

He'd point to pictures in books, to passing cars and rolling clouds, breaking waves and smiling faces, and say "Whazat?" over and over, even when he knew the answers.

I watched those hands learn to catch crawdads and lizards and pop flies and bounce passes; to do homework and science projects and mow the lawn and walk the dog and deliver newspapers in the pouring rain.

I saw them hit a grand slam; dunk a basketball; shoot a game-winning free throw; and pin a corsage on a girl.

I heard them play Bach in a piano recital; beat on the bathroom door to persuade his sister to come out; and clap longer, harder, and louder than anyone else, when his mom won a writing award.

I felt those hands holding mine when we crossed busy streets, said grace at dinner, or arm wrestled to prove who was stronger.

And I felt them two years ago, holding me up and keeping me strong at the memorial service after his dad died of cancer.

Now they are holding me once again, only this time, we are dancing, and I am laughing and he is wearing a wedding ring.

While his bride and her father waltz circles around us, the boy is leading me slowly about the room to an old song I first heard in high school. It's called "Last Dance" and it is almost too lovely to bear, but it is fitting for this occasion.

Because one dance ends and another begins and still, oh my, how the music plays on.

Touched by a Lawyer (Named "Ed")
- October 13, 2000 -

I swore I'd never be a stage mother. You know how they are—always bragging to strangers, telling anybody who will listen about their son, who isn't a real doctor, but plays one on TV?

I think that kind of behavior is tacky. Or I did, until my oldest landed a part in a TV series.

Now I go around cornering strangers, telling anybody who will listen about my son, who isn't a real doctor, but plays one on TV.

Tacky or not, I refuse to call it bragging. My granddaddy always said that bragging isn't bragging if you've got the truth to back it up. And that is the truth, so help me, though I find it hard to believe.

If you don't believe me, check it out. Please. And tell your friends.

What? I thought you'd never ask. The show is called "Ed." It premieres tonight at 8 P.M. on NBC (check local listings for channels and if you aren't home, tape it, even if you have to hire a six-year-old to set your VCR.)

Basically, it's about a brilliant and very cute small-town doctor named Mike, who is a devoted husband and father, a pretty fair bowler, a walking anthology of not-so-famous quotations, and in real life, my boy Josh.

Yes, I wrote that myself.

Ed is Mike's buddy from high school, a lawyer who goes back home to practice law in a bowling alley and moves in with Mike, his lovely wife and their adorable baby, who is not really my grandchild, but will do for now.

I don't know why they call the show "Ed." I think "Mike" sounds a lot better, don't you? Guess I shouldn't complain. They could've called it "Touched by a Lawyer."

My son insists he is not the star of the show, that it's really about Ed, not Mike. Right. Whatever.

I don't care if he is the star or not. I'm just thankful that he has benefits. Who needs stardom when you've got medical and dental?

Besides, what the boy doesn't realize is how much fun we're all having—his family and friends and even folks he doesn't know—cheering him on from the wings.

Like his cousins in the Carolinas who have hunted down and fought like badgers for every issue of every magazine that so much as mentions his name.

And my sister, a nurse in an intensive care unit, who insists on telling her patients all about him before she gives them their meds.

And the guys in the shop where he rented a tuxedo, who promised to watch the show and want him to come back when he gets famous and can afford to buy a tux.

And the manager of a restaurant where he bused dishes in high school, who said she gets goose bumps thinking about it and "It couldn't happen to a nicer guy."

And my brother, who is blind, but will "watch" every episode and spot the boy instantly by his voice.

And all the family, friends, and even strangers who celebrated recently when he married the girl of his dreams—the people who watched him as he grew up, played basketball, graduated from college, lost his dad to cancer, and found his way in the world. They'll all be pulling for him tonight.

Sometimes, when the world gets to be a bit much and the bad news starts to outweigh the good, I like to take all the kindnesses I've been shown in my life and drop them like silver dollars on the scale.

I like to think about the amazing capacity, an endless supply of grace that people have to feel for one another—to bear burdens and share sorrows and celebrate joys—and to listen to a woman brag about her son, who is not a real doctor, but plays one on TV.

Which is not to suggest that you should watch the show—but there could be a quiz on it later.

Stay tuned. If it gets canceled, I'll tell you where to write.

Spilled Milk
- November 2, 2000 -

Not counting the hot spot gas station on the highway, or the Frosty Cone stand that's only open in summer, there are now a dozen or so eating establishments in my hometown. And as I recall, there used to be just one: home.

Not only does it make dining out possible, it makes deciding where to eat an argument. Especially among strong-minded women.

This evening, there are four of us in that fray. I vote for something light, maybe just a salad, because not only am I health conscious, but I had two Hardee's biscuits for breakfast and a box of Krispy Kreme donuts for lunch.

My vote, however, doesn't count for much because even though I grew up in this town, I am now only a guest, an infrequent visitor from California, who can't be trusted to know grits from sushi.

Jane, my best friend from high school, is partial to the restaurant that always features fried chicken. Actually, all Southern restaurants tend to feature fried chicken, but her favorite also features fried trout, fried shrimp, and fried ham.

My sister Bobbie prefers a pizza place where you can get a bucket of pasta, several loaves of garlic bread, and meatballs so big you have to eat them with a forklift.

Then there's Kiowa, Bobbie's four-year-old granddaughter, who flat out refuses to eat anywhere unless it has French fries on the menu and horse pictures on the wall.

Fortunately, the only place that is open tonight happens to have plenty of both. So Kiowa gets her French fries. We get prime rib. I also get a salad. It's good.

Pretty soon the conversation turns to the good old days, the way things were way back when, and how much they've changed.

"Wait a minute," I say, suddenly recognizing the building housing the restaurant. "This was the old Five & Dime! When I was little, I used to bring $5 in here and do all my Christmas shopping."

"I know," Bobbie says. "This is where you bought Mama that godawful 'Blue Waltz' perfume."

She never lets me live that down. OK, so here's the story. One summer—after I blew 20 percent of my Christmas budget to get my mother the finest perfume a dollar could buy—my brother Joe and I got into a little altercation in the back of the car and accidentally broke a gallon jar of milk.

My mother said, "God help us!"

I said, "I didn't do it!"

Joe said, "Lord have mercy, this car is gonna stink to high heaven!"

And so it did. My mother tried everything to get rid of the stench, but sour milk smells worse than a rabid skunk. Finally in desperation my stepfather doused the back seat with her bottle of "Blue Waltz."

Which combined with the sour milk to create an entirely new odor unlike any ever known to man. It was so bad we had to ride with our heads hanging out the windows like a family of cocker spaniels.

As I tell the story, I notice that Kiowa hangs on the words the way a four-year-old will when she wants to remember something forever.

I remember hearing my parents and grandparents tell such stories—stories of what we like to call the good old days, when in truth, they weren't always so good.

I have never been big on plastic, but I have to tell you, I

consider it a godsend to be able to buy milk in an unbreakable container.

Whenever I go back to visit my hometown, it takes my breath away to realize how fast things are changing, how rapidly the old is making way for the new.

I'm glad to see the restaurants, the book and the antique shops, and the plans to build a new library. I love how they are renovating, more than just tearing down.

But I hope they will be careful, that they'll invest the time and the effort and the money to do it right, and recognize what's at stake.

Maybe there's no point in crying over spilled milk. But once it sours, there's no prettying it up.

Ain't She Somethin'
- December 12, 2000 -

M Y daughter is graduating from college this week. Yes, thank you, there is a God in Heaven. The day Nan was born, fat and round and lovelier by far than the moon and all its stars, I held her close, felt the beat of her heart and whispered in her tiny velvet ear.

"I'm your mother," I said. "I'll try my best to help you grow up to be the woman I see in your eyes." Then I pledged a solemn vow.

"I promise that I will never try to relive my life through yours."

OK, so, on that last part I lied. It was not the only promise I ever failed to keep. But I did try my very best to help her grow up. What more can a mother do?

Well, friends, what I am doing this morning—and have been doing off and on for several days—is trying to keep a promise I made to her some years ago when her brother graduated from college. I am not what you would call craftsy. But I did a fair job, if I do say so myself, in putting together a scrapbook for the boy, filled with columns that I had written about him over the years.

"If I graduate from college," said his sister, in the bathroom after the ceremony as I scrubbed mascara off my face, "will you promise to give me a scrapbook too? And a BMW and a trip to Europe?"

"That's 'when' you graduate," I said, laughing, "not 'if.' And yes, I promise you'll get a scrapbook." I remember thinking there was no hurry. I'd have years to finish her scrapbook. I could do it just so, get it just right, not slap it together the way I did her brother's. Funny, isn't it? We always think we'll have lots of time to make scrapbooks and keep promises and watch children grow up. Then we turn around and scratch our heads and wonder where the time went. So here I am on deadline for my daughter's graduation, slapping together her scrapbook. I pulled a dozen or so of the columns I wrote about her over the years. They recall memories such as these:

> When she was three, she loved to host tea parties and would insist that I—or her dad or her brothers or the mailman or the dog—had to stop whatever we were doing and sit down at her table for "tea." When she was five, she'd come home from kindergarten bringing me lovely bouquets of flowers she stole from the neighbors' yards. When she was seven, she wrote a poem that said I was the "bestest mom in

*the whole world." And when she was 18, she told me that I should
get a life and get my nose out of hers.*

Every graduation has its own meaning and importance, not
just for the graduates, but for their parents, especially if it means
that instead of paying tuition, they can now afford to buy shoes.
But my daughter's graduation is of particular significance, both to
her and to me. When she totters across a stage this week in that
goofy cap and gown and a pair of six-inch heels to receive a hard-
earned B.S. in administration of justice, she will become the first
woman on either side of her lineage to graduate from college.

My mother would say, "Well, ain't that something?"

She is something, my daughter—very much the woman I saw
in her newborn eyes and every bit the person I hoped that she
would be.

She has earned her degree all on her own. But when she
receives it this week, she'll be carrying on her shoulders the hopes
and dreams of a great many people: grandparents and great-
grandparents she never met. Teachers and coaches and family
friends who believed in her and prayed for her all of her life. Her
dad, who never had the slightest doubt that she would finish college, even after he knew that he would never live to see it. And
her mother, who promised her that, no matter what, she would
always be proud of her. And that's a promise I will keep.

Call Me Mama

Tomorrow is my daughter-in-law's birthday. She married my son just four months ago, but I've known her nearly three years. It shouldn't be hard to decide on a gift for her, but somehow I can't make up my mind. Also, I'm not sure how I ought to sign her birthday card. I don't want to use my given name, because I think that would sound as if I were only a friend, and I hope to be more than that.

I think of her as my daughter. With her, that's an easy thing to do. But it doesn't seem quite right to refer to myself as her mother. For one thing, she has a mother, a lovely one at that. Besides, you don't get to be somebody's mother simply by marriage. You have to earn that title over the years.

It helps, of course, if you remember to send birthday gifts on time. As I would have, if I could have decided what to give her. The problem is not a matter of coming up with ideas. I have lots of those. I can tell you all kinds of things that I know she would like.

A handful of seashells I could gather, just for her, at the beach.

Some old snapshots of her new husband when he was just a baby.

An antique teacup handed down from a grandmother she never met.

A classic novel or an Etta James CD or five-pound bag of jelly beans.

She likes life—in all its glory, all it shapes and colors and tastes and smells. It isn't hard to find gifts for her. The trick is choosing just one.

And then there are all those things that I would like to give her, if only they were mine to give. I would start by giving her a perfect day, which means—while she is working on one coast and he is working on the other—a day they could spend together.

A long, lazy day with nothing to do and no distracting phone calls, not even from her mother-in-law. A day to sleep late and go out for pancakes, maybe see a movie (one of her choosing, not his), have afternoon tea at a fancy hotel or take a walk hand in hand on the beach. Then get all dressed up to look so fine and make a grand entrance at her favorite restaurant and turn every head in the place.

I'd make sure she got lots of cards and gifts from all her friends and family, especially her new in-laws, who mean well, but tend to be forgetful. I would give her all the time in the world for quiet thoughts and bold dreams and happy anticipations; and lots of chances to see that little wicked blue light that always shines in her husband's eyes when he's about to say something goofy.

I would give her a mirror in which she would forever see herself, inside and out, as the true beauty that she is. I would buy her a gift certificate to have children someday, but only when she is ready to be a mother, and he is ready to be a dad. And I would give her 75 years or so to be happily married to my boy. If only it were mine to give.

Instead, I will send her flowers. And a birthday cake. And a card that will be late, but nonetheless well intentioned. And I will sign it the way I sign birthday cards for her husband: "Happy birthday. So glad you were born. I love you—Mama"

Mama assumes neither the formality of Mother, nor the familiarity of Mom.

It's not half as frumpy as Mother-in-Law. And it is not what she calls her mother.

Mama is the name her husband always calls me when that blue light starts shining in his eyes.

And maybe someday if I am lucky and don't forget her birthday too often, she just might like to call me that, too.

A Pretty Big Birthday
- February 15, 2001 -

When I was little, I took it as my appointed duty to let everybody know, lest anyone forget, that my birthday was coming soon.

I would go around for weeks in advance announcing to anybody who was willing to listen, "I'm only six now, and that's still little, but I'll be seven soon, and that's big, so you don't want to forget."

I did this primarily to benefit my mother, rest her soul, who meant well but tended to be somewhat forgetful, especially when life wasn't treating her kindly, which was pretty much all the time. Even at her worst, given enough notice, she could usually manage to bake me a cake—the best cake you would ever put in your mouth.

I also did it to help my dad, bless his heart, who would never intentionally forget my birthday but might on occasion if not forewarned forget to inquire as to what I might like for a gift. And then I'd end up having to settle for something that he won playing numbers on the punchboard, which generally meant either a wooden jewelry box filled with stale chocolates or a colorful assortment of fishing lures. The chocolates weren't so bad. And the jewelry boxes made fine caskets for burying small pets.

I would further announce my coming birthday to my teachers. (Especially the one who was so forgetful she came to school one dark, stormy day wearing nothing but a pair of rain boots and a slip. Rumor tried to make it a half slip, but it was whole. The woman was forgetful, not crazy.)

If the teacher remembered what I'd been telling her for weeks (or saw the reminders I wrote on the blackboard) she would have my classmates sing "Happy Birthday" to me. And I would blush beet red and act entirely surprised.

I never thought of it as acting. I just thought I was being helpful. Some people need reminding. It would prove to be excellent training for my 30-year marriage to a high school coach who would never have forgotten my birthday, he said, had I not had the nerve to be born during basketball season.

"My birthday is coming soon," I would tell him. "I'm only 19 now (or 29 or 39) and that's still little, but soon I'm going to be 20 (or 30 or 40) and that's pretty big, so you'd best not forget."

Usually, that was enough to jog his memory, so I rarely had to resort to more drastic measures, such as unplugging the scoreboard during one of his games. After a lifetime of not-so-gentle reminders, he got pretty good at remembering my birthday. In his last years, as cancer and chemo ravaged his body and mind, he still seldom forgot me at all.

The year he died, two weeks before I turned 50, I forgot all about my birthday. I doubt I'd have remembered it at all, had my children not reminded me.

"Mom," they said, "your birthday's coming and like it or not, we're going to celebrate."

That was three years ago—three long years of ups and downs, moving forward and letting go, feeling little and trying to be big. And here is one of several things that I have learned. You don't need to remind others to celebrate your birthday. You just need to remember to celebrate it yourself—to be glad to be alive and to live well.

My birthday is coming soon. I'll be 53, which is pretty darn big, and I intend to celebrate it. That's the reason I'm writing this—because I want you to know I'll be taking a week-long vacation from writing stories—and not because I want you to remember my birthday.

Unless you really want to.

Not Just Brothers
- April 10, 2001 -

They were born five years apart, looking almost identical— pink, hairless, and helpless as baby rats—with a sister in between to referee. All their lives, I prayed for them the prayer that mothers have been praying for their sons ever since Eve gave birth to Cain and Abel—that they would grow up to be, not just brothers, but friends.

I mean this literally. Every night after I tucked them in bed—that is, after I got them to eat their broccoli, persuaded them to do their homework, demanded that they take their baths, insisted that they brush their teeth, begged them to be kind and gentle with each other, and threatened them with more plagues than it took to get the Israelites out of Egypt if they didn't go to sleep or else—I would slip into my bedroom, fall down on my knees and say, "Dear God, please let them be friends some day, and thank you that they haven't killed each other yet." I also prayed that they would never have to go to war, which seems strangely ironic, in that they were always at war with each other. Perhaps I shouldn't say always. But I don't know what else to call it. They fought day and night, except when they were asleep or apart, at which times I can assure you that they were either dreaming about fighting or planning their next fight. Coyote and Roadrunner had nothing on those two. Which is not to say they hated each other. Far from it. They were absolutely devoted in a twisted sort of way. You might even say that they were friends. Just not the kind of friends you or I would ever want.

They could play together for hours, building forts or shooting hoops or teasing their sister, before deciding to beat each other to a pulp. The age difference didn't matter; one was bigger, but the other was faster. Also, to compensate for his size, the "baby," as his older brother called him, employed a technique whereby he would lie on his back and flail his arms and legs, making it almost impossible to touch him. He could do this for hours. They called it the "dying cricket." I think they got it from watching pro wrestling on TV. Not that I ever let them watch that stuff.

Anyhow, the fights worked like this. One of them would "start it." Never mind who, they took turns. Then, when the other one fired a preemptive strike, their sister would scream, "I'M GONNA TELL MOM ON YOU GUYS!" At which time, I would dress in full riot gear, rush in like a SWAT team, back them into corners and try once again to remind the little hellions that brothers are meant to be brothers—to look out for each other, to stick together come what may, to be best friends, not worst nightmares.

They never listened. The fighting changed somewhat as they grew older. Instead of pounding each other with fists, they battled it out at basketball or Nintendo or Connect-Four. Less bloody, but just as fierce. Their sister still had to referee.

It would've happened sooner or later, no doubt, even if they hadn't lost their dad. Boys grow up for all sorts of reasons, who's to say why or when. But when you lose someone you love—someone so strong and steadfast you were sure he'd be around forever—it makes you think about things like the meaning of life and the whimsy of fate and the preciousness of the people you hold dear. When their dad died three years ago, my boys not only became men, they became friends.

Last fall when the oldest got married his brother was his best man. And this morning I took the best man to the airport to fly to New York to spend a week with his brother, who's not a real doctor but plays one on TV.

It's a fine and lovely thing, an answer to a mother's prayers, to see boys grow up to be men and brothers turn out to be friends. Especially if they remember to call their mother.

Never Say Never
- May 24, 2001 -

My grandmother used to say that you should never say never, because never is a very long time.

I never was sure what she meant.

I remember once, years ago, having an argument with my husband about some people he thought we ought to spend more time with. Never mind who.

"I am never going anywhere with them again," I told him.

"You don't mean that," he said.

"I do too mean it!" I snapped. "They are rude, self-centered, and vulgar! The next time one of them tells me to pull his finger, I'm going to rip it right off his hand!"

"OK, I know they can act like jerks sometimes," he said, "but, hey, they're our children."

Every time I got in a car with those three I swore I'd never do it again. And every time I broke that vow they had the nerve to laugh.

The one part of those road trips that I always loved was getting to drive late at night, after the kids and their father all fell asleep.

I had this little routine. First, I would switch the radio to play my music, not theirs, very softly lest, God forbid, I wake them up. Then I would pop open a Diet Pepsi, crack the window for air, prop my left foot on the dashboard, rest my right foot on the gas, and drive along for hours keeping one eye on the road and the other on the rearview mirror, where I could see their faces—eyes shut tight, mouths wide open, drool dripping off their chins.

And I would feel as happy as I had ever felt and remind myself to never say never, because never is a very long time.

Then one day, I found myself blinking into the sun—as if I'd just crawled out of a cave where I had been in hibernation—and realized that my children had all grown up, my husband had died and I was taking road trips alone.

My driving routine was still the same, except now I could play music as loud as I pleased and all I could see in the rear view mirror were headlights and memories.

I was thinking about that last weekend, driving back from San Francisco. My oldest, who is not a real doctor but plays one on TV, scored tickets to see the Dave Matthews Band at PacBell Park and offered to take me—along with his wife and his brother and sister—as a late Mother's Day gift.

I insisted that we all go in one car together so we could "visit" on the two-hour drive to the concert.

I don't know why I did that. My boys aren't just big; they're huge. They need separate cars for their feet. And while my daughter and daughter-in-law are tiny, they do not like being crowded, they hate getting carsick, and they are not keen on taking a backseat.

"I'll never insist on taking one car again," I said. "You guys can go in one and I'll drive myself."

And they had the nerve to laugh.

But I loved the concert. I loved seeing my oldest be gracious with strangers who shouted, "'Ed' is my favorite show!" and asked him to pose for pictures.

I loved hearing my daughter admit that I was right and thank me for making her bring a jacket.

I loved looking down the row and seeing beside me four of the most gorgeous faces God ever put on this earth, and kicking myself for not bringing a camera.

I loved walking out in a sea of 40,000 people, all desperate to find a bathroom, and being flanked by "bodyguards": my oldest in front, parting the crowd ("Mom, hang onto my jacket!") and my youngest in back, keeping us close ("Mom, don't wander off!").

What? Yes, of course, I loved the music. That electric fiddle player was enough to make me forget the names of my children.

But the part I loved best was driving home that night while my kids all were sleeping. I looked at their faces—eyes shut, mouths open, drool dripping off their chins—and felt as happy as I have ever felt. And I reminded myself to never say never.

Because never is a very long time.

Afterword

On Writing

People often ask what advice I have for someone who wants to be a writer. They assume because I write for a living, I ought to be able to tell others how to do it.

It's a fair assumption. But the truth is, asking me how to write is like asking directions from a blind man with a seeing-eye dog; I don't know how to tell you the way to get there. I just follow the dog. That said, here are a few tricks the dog keeps trying to teach me.

First, write about what you know, the thing that's right in front of you, the thing you've been given to write about, the thing you can't seem to get off your mind.

Read everything you can find by the writers you like best; if you like them, it's probably because their voice speaks to the voice in you. Develop that voice. It's yours.

Write like yourself, the way you talk. Read what you've written out loud. If it doesn't sound like you, rewrite it until it does.

Learn the rules of writing and stick to them a long time before you dare start messing around. Write between the lines; say more with less. And be prepared to suffer, not because writing invites heartache, but because it always insists on examining it.

Never pretend to be what you aren't, or to know what you don't know. That applies to life more than to writing, maybe, but the two are not so different. And as for inspiration, I don't need it to write. I just need a deadline. Surest cure I've ever found for writer's block.

If you want to write, if you feel called to do so, you should. And you will. Maybe you won't earn a living at it. Few writers ever do. But you can write cards to encourage the downhearted;

and notes of condolences to comfort those who suffer loss; and crisp, compelling business letters that clearly explain why the item you received was not the item you ordered, and what exactly you will do if you are not reimbursed.

You can write grant applications and memos to colleagues and letters to the editor, or to your congressman, or to God, to shed light and right wrongs and make the world a better place, or at least, to get a load off your chest.

You can write for posterity the stories your grandparents told you, stories that will be lost if you don't write them before you die.

You can write love letters to your children or to anyone, really, to say all the things that you could never say with your mouth.

You can even write in a journal, if you are so inclined (and a lot more disciplined than I am) to get to know yourself better.

That, of course, is the real reason we read and write—to know and to be known. It has been that way a very long time and I expect it always will. It works like this.

You take thoughts and feelings from your mind and your heart, and occasionally from your soul, and you fashion them into words. That is called language.

You put the words on paper, or perhaps on a computer screen, using lines and circles, marks and symbols, until you trust them to carry your meaning. That is called writing.

Then someone, who perhaps has never seen your face or heard your voice, sees your lines and circles and symbols and marks, and recognizes them as words. That is called reading.

Sometimes, unpredictably, the words hold the power to recreate the writer's thoughts and feelings in the mind and the heart and even in the soul of the reader.

That is called a miracle.

Some do it for love. Some do it for money. And some of us, if we are lucky, get to do it for both. And that's where I will stop for now. The dog has gone to sleep.

Four-Mile Stretches

[*Note: This column also appeared in a slightly expanded version in* Reader's Digest.]

From where I live on the tip of California's Monterey Peninsula, there is no easy way to get anywhere.

To go north, for instance, from my house to San Francisco, you take Highway 1, also known as the scenic Old Coast Highway, and proceed to 101, also known as the Freeway from Hell.

Most of that route, whether scenic or hellacious, is a multilane, divided road, which depending on weather and traffic, can either take you where you're going or drive you out of your mind. Sometimes it does both.

The part I dread most—or did at one time—is a two-lane stretch of 156 that connects Highways 1 and 101.

In the South, where I grew up, such roads are called "cow trails" partly because they are frequented by farm equipment and other slow-moving vehicles that trot along, nose to tail, at bovine speed; and also because if you get on such a road, you'll be on it until the cows come home. So to speak.

In some ways, roads are like people; they have "personalities" that can be shaped and colored by how we see them, how we feel about them. I first realized this when my husband was diagnosed with cancer and we began what would be a four-year pilgrimage to Stanford Medical Center for treatment—surgeries, radiation, chemotherapy, countless appointments, and more than a few emergencies.

It was 91 miles—two hours, give or take—and I hated every inch of it, most especially, that two-lane bottleneck. I drove it so often I knew it by heart, and hated it more with each drive.

Then they started construction.

I did everything I could to avoid it. I begged and bribed to get appointments at off-peak times, only to end up stuck in rush-hour traffic on the drive home. I spent hours poring over maps and drove miles out of the way trying to get around it, only to find, one way or the other, it really didn't matter; there was no getting around it.

I had no choice but to drive it. But that didn't mean I had to like it. I'd clench my teeth, grip the wheel and feel my stomach churning for hours or even days after the drive was over.

Once, when we were running late for an appointment, I muttered under my breath, "I hate this stupid road."

I didn't think my husband could hear me. Morphine is great for pain, but it doesn't do much for conversation.

"Four miles," he said.

I looked over. His eyes were closed.

"What did you say?" I asked.

"This part of the road," he said, with his teaching voice, as if lecturing his high school physics students. "It's only four miles long. That's easy. You can do anything for four miles."

I clocked it. He was right. Four miles exactly. I could have sworn it was 20.

Suddenly that drive got easier. I don't mean it seemed easier; I mean it was.

Four miles was not just doable, but entirely understandable. That was the distance we used to walk together from our house to the beach and back. It was half the length of a trail he loved to hike in Yosemite, even with a baby on his back; four times as long as a walk to the park to play catch with our kids; and a mere fraction of the 26 miles he once ran in the Big Sur Marathon.

Four miles was nothing; nothing to complain about, and nothing to waste when he had only months to live.

So I stopped complaining and started looking to see what I could see. And suddenly, there were acres of artichoke fields. And an old barn reflected on a mirror-like pond. Roadside stalls selling strawberries and flowers. And a white horse standing guard on a hill.

Those things were there all along, probably. I just never noticed. But I notice them now, every chance I get. I see new things everywhere I go.

Sometimes, when the road ahead seems longer and harder than I want it to be, I try to break it up into pieces in my mind and in my heart and even in my soul—I divide it up into four-mile stretches and take them one at a time.

Some roads can seem impassable.

But you can do anything for four miles.

Made in the USA
Lexington, KY
12 February 2012